Early Islamic Syria

BRISTOL CLASSICAL PRESS DEBATES

Series editor: Richard Hodges

Early Islamic Syria

AN ARCHAEOLOGICAL
ASSESSMENT

Alan Walmsley

Bristol Classical Press

Published by Bristol Classical Press 2012

Bristol Classical Press, an imprint of Bloomsbury Publishing Plc

Bloomsbury Publishing Plc
50 Bedford Square
London WC1B 3DP
www.bloomsburyacademic.com

Copyright © Alan Walmsley 2007

First published by Gerald Duckworth & Co. Ltd. 2007

The author has asserted his rights under the Copyright, Designs and
Patents Act 1988 to be identified as the author of this work.

ISBN: 978 0 715 63570 4

A CIP catalogue record for this book is available from the British Library

Typeset by Ray Davies
Printed and bound in Great Britain by CPI Bath

Contents

For my mother, Violet
and in memory of my father, George

List of Illustrations

Preface

In this book I endeavour to offer a concise account of Islamic archaeology as it has developed and is today in the region of geographical Syria-Palestine. For any book that purports to deal with current issues in archaeology, this region is unsurpassed. Even choosing a name by which to describe the region is problematic, and exposes compelling current political tensions. In this work 'Syria-Palestine' is used to describe the area covered by the modern states of Syria, Lebanon, Jordan, Israel and the Palestinian territories, with a small part of southern Turkey, but should not be viewed as expressing any other opinion. The term is an old one for the region, but is the best, given current circumstances. 'The Levant' was another option, but it can be awkward to use in writing and is compromised by its past use as a cultural term, sometimes pejoratively. As this book sets out to counter earlier judgemental approaches to the archaeology of Islamic Syria-Palestine, the term 'The Levant' seemed particularly inappropriate.

While setting geographical parameters can be difficult and fraught, the region offers the archaeologist particular attractions in dealing with an Islamic past as a result of the tremendous advances made in relevant archaeological research in the last few decades. A virtual explosion in discovery and interpretation has characterised the field since the 1980s in particular, in which archaeological-anthropological approaches have come to supplement, then become independent of, and, more recently, supplant traditional art historical and architectural studies. At the same time, a profound change has also occurred in the study of Islamic art and architecture, two developments that feed on and encourage each other. It has produced a dynamic and exciting field for modern research, glimpses into which are attempted in this book.

The reader will find that recent archaeological discoveries in Jordan feature predominantly in this study. That is not surprising, given the great interest shown by Jordanian scholars and international missions in the exploration of that country's Islamic heritage, and the fact that much of my own research has been conducted there. Likewise work in Syria by local and international missions has promoted the study of Islamic archaeology in that country, both formative projects in the 1960s and 70s and more recent, scientifically advanced ventures. Significant discoveries have also occurred in other countries in the region, and together they allow new approaches with which to describe and interpret Islamic society, especially in the formative early centuries. Now is certainly an exciting time to be an Islamic archaeologist at work in the Middle East, given not only the rapid advance of the subject in the region but also the modern world's desperate need to understand and build dialogue between Anglo-European society and Islamic countries. This book makes a small contribution by trying to challenge a number of misconceptions about Islamic history found in earlier Western scholarship, misconceptions still invoked today in debates over past relations between Christians, Muslims and Jews. By applying new archaeological data one can question and often counter many of the basic tenets of these misconceptions. In their place this work proposes new ways of understanding and interpreting the first Islamic centuries in Syria-Palestine, based on clear and verifiable information gleaned from a range of archaeological discoveries made in recent decades. The reader is introduced to many of the issues and the range and value of the material that can be applied to them in Chapter 1.

Current debates in the archaeology of early Islamic Syria-Palestine are presented from two perspectives in this book. The first considers mostly long-standing questions that have, and continue to be, dealt with by a chronological-historical approach; that is, issues that are treated within specific time periods such as the sixty years before the Islamic expansion, the decades of the expansion itself, or events that relate to the first two dynasties (the Umayyad, 660-750 CE and Abbasid, after 750; see Appendix 1). Such issues are normally treated within a conventional chronological framework, and tend to hang on major historical events – the Islamic 'conquest', Umayyad dynastic feuds, and the overthrow of the Umayyads in 750, in particular. While this book does not, in any way, endorse a continuing reliance on dynastic frameworks for research into the archaeology of the early Islamic period – and indeed the intention is quite the opposite – Chapter 2 focuses on a prominent historically-oriented debate that has prevailed in Islamic archaeology until today; namely, socio-economic conditions in Syria-Palestine on the eve of the Islamic expansion.

The other approach, by way of contrast, attempts to move beyond this increasingly outdated and inappropriate model to potentially more useful ones that tackle the major debates head-on; this can be defined as issues-based archaeology and sets the tone for the rest of the book. Chapter 3 focuses on material culture, Chapter 4 on critical questions of settlement profiles, and Chapter 5 on resultant socio-economic issues relevant to the whole period. The purpose of such an approach is to challenge artificially imposed historical boundaries and to deal with society as an organic, developing entity. Theoretically, the approach is from the perspective of the *longue durée* (structural continuity from a macro-historical perspective), unconstrained by a simplistic 'cause and effect' syndrome programmed on a passive population by a series of unrelated historical events. Implications of this approach for current and future Islamic archaeology in Syria-Palestine are treated in the concluding chapter.

There is no doubt that this book is a fusion of material and ideas that I have had the privilege to assemble over the last three decades from many friends and colleagues, both within the Middle East and outside it. They are too many to mention individually, but it would be inappropriate not to mention a few influential individuals who encouraged me in my earlier years, for their influence can be seen throughout this study. As always, they are in no way responsible for the views expressed in this book and, I am sure, will not agree with much, if any, of it. However, they can claim as much credit as they wish.

Perhaps the easiest way is to mention them is in the order in which, from memory, I met them: the late Tony (A.W.) McNicoll, who steered me towards Islamic archaeology and encouraged, if not compelled, me to question ideas then current; Crystal Kessler, whose enthusiasm for Islamic architecture was infectious; Alastair Northedge, who gave me my first and unforgettable taste of Islamic archaeology; Ghazi Bisheh, a profound influence and perceptive mind; Ahmad Shboul, friend, colleague and insightful Islamic historian who embraces with enthusiasm the potential contribution of archaeology to Islamic studies; Don Whitcomb, who taught me the vital and creative combination of fact and vision; Cherie Lenzen, who emphasised the need to step outside the accepted; Jeremy Johns, who can see the unseen; and Alison McQuitty, encouraging and questioning in always the kindest ways, but no less effectively. Thanks.

These are some of the people who had a significant and enduring influence on my early work. Since then many others have both encouraged and challenged me, and to them also goes my gratitude. While they are too many to name, I have benefited enormously from discussions with my postgraduate students at Copenhagen University. I must thank also Richard

Hodges for twisting my arm just enough to write this slim volume and Deborah Blake at Duckworth for being so incredibly patient with me finishing it. My final thanks must go to the people of Jordan, and especially to my friends and colleagues in the Department of Antiquities. It has been thirty years since my first, exhilarating visit to their country. Each time I return the thrill is still there; few places can match that.

This book, then, is a synthesis of ideas and approaches garnered over a number of years from numerous influences. Its intention is to challenge many old interpretations that are increasingly seen as misguided and, in their place, proffers new explanations; whether they are equally inadequate only time will tell.

Copenhagen and Amman, 2006

A note on the writing of Arabic names

For ease of reading, no diacritical marks have been used in this book. Italicised Arabic words are explained in the Glossary. As some Arabic terms are difficult to translate accurately they have been retained in the body of the text.

1

Defining Islamic archaeology in Syria-Palestine

The origins and development of a branch of archaeology that focuses specifically on Islamic periods and Islamic lands spans more than a century, but as with other areas of archaeological research improvements have been especially rapid in the last two or three decades (the literature is growing, but see especially Grabar 1976; Northedge 1999; Petersen 2005b; Rogers 1974; Vernoit 1997; Walmsley 2004). In the last century, many of the issues facing Islamic archaeology have been the same as those confronting other archaeologies, and continue to be so while the field diversifies. Specifically, Islamic archaeology has had to get to grips with building a working relationship with the broader field of Islamic studies, seeking common theoretical and methodological approaches with other branches of archaeology, coming to understand what Islamic archaeology – as an archaeology of historical periods – can and cannot do and, lastly, mapping possible future developments in the field. These issues are tackled to some extent in this chapter, drawing upon examples from work in Syria-Palestine over the last hundred years, while the last question is the subject of Chapter 6.

The historical origins of Islamic archaeology in Syria-Palestine have inevitably shaped its development and influenced its status today. Early studies in the first half of the twentieth century focused almost exclusively on standing architecture, perhaps overly so, but had the advantage of rapidly promoting the field as a legitimate and worthwhile area of academic research. The prevalence of architectural studies can be traced back to ground-breaking work in the field, notably the discoveries in the late nineteenth and early twentieth centuries by pioneering explorers such as Alois Musil (1907a, 1907b), Rudolf Brünnow and Alfred von Domaszewski (1904-9), and Antonin Jaussen and Raphaël Savignac (1909-22), which were then followed by the more analytical researches of K.A.C. Creswell and Jean Sauvaget (see below). Serving as a solid basis for later work and, in particular, providing an inspiration for later archaeological investigations, the contribution of these scholars requires a brief mention.

The exploration of Syria-Palestine and Arabia in the later nineteenth and early twentieth centuries stood apart from earlier voyages of discovery in the Middle East, in that these expeditions sought to be thoroughly accurate and comprehensive in their work by describing, mapping and photographing in detail the places visited. Earlier sources were researched, and the possible historical context of the location and buildings investigated. The publications of Alois Musil resulting from his journeys in the area of modern Jordan were outstanding in both breadth and depth of study as they included, in addition to exhaustive architectural reports, detailed geographical observations and ethnographic accounts of the nomadic tribes living in the region. Unquestionably, the highlight of his travels was the discovery of the exquisite country palace of Qusayr Amra to the east of Amman (Musil 1907a, 1907b), probably built early in the eighth century by the Umayyad caliph al-Walid (r. 705-15 – see Appendix 1 for details of the dynasties and rulers of early Islamic Syria-Palestine). This small but remarkable palace quickly received attention because of its colourful wall paintings that included among their subjects naturalistic animal and human figures, some of the latter female and scantily dressed, if clothed at all. These images were startlingly unexpected for an Islamic building, and provoked considerable interest in the architecture of the first Islamic centuries and, in particular, how it could be understood. By the end of the first quarter of the twentieth century, the large body of data generated by the publications of Musil and others on early Islamic architecture was in great need of classification and analysis. Although a daunting task, this was nevertheless undertaken by K.A.C. Creswell and completed with enormous authority.

Creswell's most enduring and influential legacy was his Penguin paperback *A Short Account of Early Muslim Architecture* (Creswell 1958), subsequently reprinted and, more recently, revised and updated by James Allan (Creswell and Allan 1989). This readily accessible book was a shortened version of Creswell's monumental *Early Muslim Architecture*, published in two volumes with volume 1 later revised in two parts (Creswell 1932, 1940, 1969). In this acknowledged masterpiece, Creswell ranged widely in his subject matter and analysis, dealing in detail with the extensive architectural heritage of the Umayyad dynasty in Syria-Palestine. Only in recent years have questions arisen as to the value of persisting with such scholarship, and major challenges been made to some of Creswell's basic tenets, such as the supposed architectural barrenness of Arabia before Islam or the proposed origin of the mosque in the House of the Prophet Muhammad in Madinah (Allan 1991; Johns 1999).

Also concerned with understanding architecture in context was the pioneering French scholar Jean Sauvaget, remembered for his work on the so-called 'Desert Castles' of the Umayyads and, especially, the Syrian cities of Aleppo, Ladhikiyah and Damascus (Sauvaget 1934; 1967). Particularly influential was his widely referenced model on the development of the 'medieval *suq*', in which Sauvaget argued that the conversion of the broad colonnaded streets of classical cities into an enclosed and covered market – a *suq*, found in every major city of Syria – occurred during a period of political upheaval beginning in the ninth century (encapsulated in Sauvaget 1934: 99-102; 1941: 104-5). As Sauvaget was dealing with still operating towns, he relied upon historical rather than archaeological evidence to date the formation of the *suq* in the Syrian cities (see, again for Aleppo, Sauvaget 1941: 83-92). According to Sauvaget, this poaching of public space, representing the uncontrolled encroachment of private structures over once wide open streets, was an outcome of the unleashing of an anarchic 'oriental' mentality after a millennium of classical civic 'order'; that is, an entirely Islamic phenomenon representing, in a physical sense, the cultural reassertion by an 'Oriental East' over an ordered, Hellenised ('Western') urban environment. His underlying social theory was one that equated political disorder with social chaos; a colonial view, one that championed and legitimised iron rule over a subject people and their perceived unruly ways. His influential model has been often repeated as evidence for urban and, indeed, cultural change in the Islamic period.

At about the same time as these early architectural and urban studies were taking shape, the first significant archaeological excavations of Islamic-period sites took place in Syria-Palestine, and even if some of the work was more accidental or simply incidental than intentional, the discoveries were intellectually challenging and could not be ignored. Khirbat Mafjar ('Hisham's Palace') on the outskirts of the oasis of Jericho in the Jordan Valley was a clear case. The large field of ruins north of the village was first interpreted as being anything from Hellenistic/Herodian to Byzantine or Crusader in date, but excavations between 1934 and 1948 under the auspices of the Palestine Department of Antiquities turned up something quite different and unexpected (Hamilton 1959; 1988). The work revealed a large monument built in four distinct parts: a walled enclosure (*qasr*), a forecourt with a fountain, a mosque (rather small) and, despite its ruined condition, an imposing reception hall with a huge floor paved with

mosaics and adjoining baths. Again, the widespread representation of human and animal figures, this time featured in
three-dimensional carved stucco decoration, in an Islamic
building invited explanation as to its inspiration and purpose,
on which debate still continues.

Excavations of major 'tells' (archaeological mounds) additionally brought Islamic-period remains to the attention of
archaeologists, but these finds were often unwanted and rarely
treated seriously. At Baysan (Beth Shan), a major complex of
early Islamic date was cleared and almost totally removed from
the summit of Tell Husn, but only scantily published (Fitzgerald 1931). Admittedly very ruined, the importance of the
discovery was nonetheless ignored, and still is, as the purpose
of the excavation was to discover the site's ancient, especially
Biblical, remains. Better implemented for the times were the
Danish excavations on the tell of Hamah in Syria, which also
uncovered extensive if often confused Islamic remains. The
recent publication of the later levels has demonstrated the
great difficulty faced by the excavators as a result of the very
mixed nature of the deposits (Pentz 1997). Subsequent excavations in Jordan of two large tell-sites located south of Amman
at Dhiban and Hisban (Heshbon) in the 1950s and from 1968
respectively revealed major Islamic deposits. While both sites
were selected because of their importance as Biblical centres, a
change in emphasis can be observed at Hisban where the
later-period ceramics, including Islamic, were used as the basis
of a doctoral thesis by James Sauer (1973). The outcome was
the emergence in Jordan of one of the first foreign archaeologists who took the material culture of the early Islamic period
seriously and sought to differentiate it from preceding Byzantine-period finds (Whitcomb 2000b).

Other early archaeological work in Syria-Palestine had as its
objective the large-scale exposure of elite buildings thought to
be Islamic in date and the salvaging of the architectural deco-

ration they contained, such as stucco, mosaics and paintings. While this might have been a reasonable objective, given archaeological standards in the mid-twentieth century, little attention was paid to the contents of the excavated rooms, or the wider context of the monuments. The result was often stunning discoveries and comprehensive architectural reports, but somewhat vacant occupational histories devoid of any human presence. For instance, excavations in the 1930s of the Umayyad 'desert palace' of Qasr al-Hayr al-Gharbi uncovered remarkable painted floors, on which human and animal subjects were depicted, and extensive stucco remains from a monumental gateway into the palace that included an almost life-size sculptured representation of the caliph, as at Khirbat al-Mafjar. While much consideration was paid to preserving and publishing the architectural features of the site – the stucco gateway was subsequently reconstructed at the National Museum in Damascus – other cultural remains received scant attention and the history of the site was reconstructed predominantly on the architectural finds. However, a more detailed occupational history that might have helped in understanding the original purpose of the building (which is not clear for many of these 'desert palaces') was as neglected as the finds from the excavation; finds that might have provided some answers to these very questions. A similar situation existed with the excavation of the mudbrick and stuccoed palaces at Raqqah in north Syria, undertaken by the Syrian Department of Antiquities between 1950 and 1954.

It is tragic that archaeological investigations at many early Islamic sites in Syria-Palestine have failed adequately to consider site settlement histories and the nature of their occupation, for instance social roles and economic activities, in some cases even after years of work. The small urban settlement of Anjar in the Biqa valley of Lebanon is a particularly notorious example. Excavations commenced at the site in 1953 as a show-piece project for the then new Lebanese Antiquities service, with research on this enigmatic site continuing on and off ever since, but with only gradual improvement in clarity (Chehab 1993; Hillenbrand 1999). At Anjar and many other sites, even when the excavations had an Islamic focus, the emphasis was on cities and monuments. The goal of many projects was the hasty exposure of architecture, with little interest in understanding 'minor details' such as settlement histories, the cultural environment, or economic systems; with some projects it is doubtful if such objectives – today an important part of archaeological research – were understood at all. Nevertheless, until the mid-twentieth century these early projects did lay the foundations for, and did much to draw attention to, Islamic archaeology as a legitimate field of study. In addition to the burst of architectural discoveries in Syria-Palestine datable to the Umayyad dynasty, which required Creswell to publish a revised and considerably expanded volume 1 of his *Early Muslim Architecture* (Creswell 1969), these excavations at sites such as Mafjar and Raqqah helped to establish a fledgling reference corpus of early Islamic ceramics, but due to the lower priority placed on ceramic studies the misdating of the finds was a common problem (for example at Mafjar; see Whitcomb 1988b).

The often chance encounter with early Islamic material by a growing number of excavation projects in the mid-twentieth century led to a consideration by some archaeologists as to the nature of Islamic settlement in Syria-Palestine following the Islamic expansion of the early seventh century. It became apparent to them that a commonly accepted view current at that time of a violent and destructive conquest by mindless 'Muslim hordes' (as they were often portrayed) was quite wrong, as many sites revealed continuity of occupation and that, in fact, the arrival of Islam in the towns and countryside of Syria-Palestine was archaeologically invisible. The concept of

a brutal and devastating Islamic 'conquest' resulting in permanent cultural and economic collapse emerged in nineteenth-
century scholarship, and was widely believed well into the
twentieth century. Early explorers travelled through empty
landscapes filled with deserted ruins and brooded on the fate of
peoples and civilisations past. For Melchior de Vogüé (1865) to
Selah Merrill (1881) and, into the twentieth century, Gertrude
Bell (1907) and Rose Macaulay (1953), the only possible explanation that came to mind was rapacious Arabs, the antithesis
of an ordered, civilised life, repeatedly unleashed by the anarchic desert on the civility of the sown lands, and finally
overwhelming them. Christians, their churches and even their
supposed preference for wine were often identified as the
targets of an Arab/Muslim (the two were often seen as synonymous) 'invasion' and occupation (Negev 1974: 414; 1997: 9).
Thus Yohanan Aharoni (1964: 91) dogmatically asserted about
the church at Ramat Rahel in Palestine:

> Upon the fruit of all this zeal for building there descended
> in the seventh century the Arab invasion, which – on our
> tell as everywhere else – brought to a swift end the life of the
> Christian communities. So there came to an end, for the Holy
> Land, a chapter of its history which in our own time the
> archaeologist seeks so far as may be to bring to life.

Writers like Aharoni, shackled by their cultural partiality,
imagined with fear and trepidation the abrupt end to civilised
life and the brutal demise of a Christian Holy Land in the face
of an 'Arab invasion' and, by subtle implication, a scenario the
world faced yet again at the time of writing. Such politically-
charged messages are still being played very loudly today.

As a result of greater survey and excavation work beginning
in the 1980s at a number of major urban sites, new evidence
started to emerge that began seriously to question the reliabil-

ity of identifying the military events of the early seventh century as the single, common cause for settlement change in that century – if indeed it was a cause at all. Supposed destructions, such as that suggested for Caesarea of Palestine (Toombs 1978), were recognised as resulting from an erroneous interpretation of the archaeological data (for Caesarea, see the exemplary example of Holum 1992), based more on entrenched and mistaken Western beliefs than on a correct reading of the material evidence. Extraordinarily, the idea of a violent, vindictive conquest still persists in some literature, especially in Israel (e.g. Frankel et al. 2001: 117; Ye'or 1996: especially 43-7). Apart from these and a few other increasingly rare and outmoded examples, surely the result of academic isolation rather than prejudice, this demonstrably mistaken explanation is universally rejected today.

Another view current during the earlier part of the twentieth century attributed the perceived abandonment of sites in Syria-Palestine to economic causes, specifically severe disruptions to production and trade that resulted from the Sasanid invasion and subsequent Muslim occupation of the region in the early seventh century. Such explanations gained wide credence with the detailed and respected surveys of Howard Butler (1907-49) and Georges Tchalenko (1953-8). Their comprehensive studies of classical and post-classical architecture in Syria sought to explain why once densely populated and prosperous areas, such as the limestone hills of northwest Syria studied in detail by Tchalenko, were turned into vacant, barren wastelands. For both scholars, the change was solely attributable to historical events of the early seventh century: the Persian Sasanid occupation of the 610s followed by the Islamic (Arab) 'conquest' in the 630s. However, these events were seen as fatally undermining the once sound economic foundations of now vulnerable and impoverished rural communities, leading to flight and abandonment, rather than as a wave of destructive conquest. At least for the countryside the evidence from these surveys seemed compelling and convincing, finding wide acceptance (e.g. Brown 1971: 169). On the face of it, the postulated desertion of Syria's villages presented an east Mediterranean confirmation of Henri Pirenne's celebrated, but contested, thesis that the rapid expansion of Islam in the region resulted in a permanent disruption to once thriving Mediterranean economic networks, the sudden demise of which served as a root cause for the onset of the middle ages in the west (Pirenne 1939: 147-85; see also Delogu 1998, with essential bibliography).

If there was no conquest by 'thundering hordes' of imagined, supposedly fanatical Bedouin Arabs bursting uncontrollably out of Arabia, leaving a desolated landscape in their wake (see Silberman 2001), nor sudden economic collapse, what *was* the nature of Muslim expansion into Syria-Palestine in the early seventh century? What impact did it have on developments in socio-economic conditions and the overall vitality of local communities? In the 1950s and 1960s a new belief gained ground, one that acknowledged a smoother transition to Islam, but thereafter an overall decline in urban and rural settlement alike. The idea was first proposed following discoveries in archaeological excavations during the 1930s of an unbroken use of Christian monuments into Umayyad times, for instance at Nessana in the Negev desert of southern Palestine, and at the Jordanian sites of Jarash (Gerasa) and Mount Nebo near Madaba. The Nessana excavations between 1935 and 1937 were especially convincing, uncovering along with churches and other structures a major collection of papyri, including bilingual (Greek and Arabic) legal documents datable to the end of the seventh century (Kraemer 1958). Clearly, Islamic-period occupation of the site could not be denied, but its nature could be contested. At Mount Nebo west of Madaba, the continued use of churches was indicated by iconoclastic damage to floor mosaics, in which human and animal images were effaced but the resultant damage often carefully repaired (Saller and Schneider 1941: 106, 229-30). Likewise at Jarash images were purged from church floor mosaics, in this case with particular thoroughness (Crowfoot 1931: 4). In these early reports the erasure of images was usually attributed to the Umayyad caliphs Umar (r. 717-20) or especially Yazid II (r. 720-4), to whom an edict banning images was attributed. Muslims themselves were often imagined as carelessly, if not maliciously, scratching out the church images, thereby creating a horrible scar in the visual record that preserved for posterity the noble suffering of a subjected and persecuted people. John Crowfoot's lament on the damaged mosaics of Jarash summed it up: 'all representations of living creatures were ruthlessly destroyed. The sorry way in which the mutilations were repaired shows the wretched plight of the Christians, though it proves also that the community survived and still used the churches' (Crowfoot 1938: 172-3). The opinion was, then, that the removal of images was an eighth-century movement in Syria-Palestine, which meant that these actions offered irrefutable proof for the continued use of churches after the arrival of Islam. However, as iconoclasm was also seen as evidence for a concerted persecution of the Christian population by powerful Muslim rulers (see further below, Chapter 5, under 'Religious life'), the appearance of 'mutilated' churches in the archaeological record was often used to support the argument for urban impoverishment and cultural disintegration under Islamic rule. Unable to withstand a terminal mix of socio-religious strictures, many, if not most, urban communities declined, leaving towns 'ruralised' or abandoned by the middle of the eighth century.

With the publication in 1959 of *The Antiquities of Jordan* by Gerald Harding, Jordan's first Director-General of Antiquities, this 'devolution' model for urban society in little more than a century after the Islamic expansion became widely accepted. In Harding's view, and in that of many others that followed, the

final political and cultural marginalisation of Jordan was attributable to the overthrow of the Syrian-based Umayyad
dynasty and the subsequent anti-Umayyad policies of the Abbasid dynasty, based in Iraq. Archaeological projects in the
1960s and 1970s, especially those in Jordan and Palestine,
continued to embrace with little criticism the idea of moderate
levels of continuity after the Islamic expansion followed by
decline and final abandonment with the downfall of the
Umayyads. In many instances this explanation became a convenient and seemingly authoritative model for dealing with
material arbitrarily judged as unwanted and uninteresting by
project directors and, more influentially, the institutions that
funded them. This lack of attention was particularly sympto-
matic of projects focusing on early Christian sites, especially
where the excavation of early churches was the principal objective. Ceramic chronologies were truncated, sometimes severely
so, to accommodate a shortened time span, in which much later
material was compacted into the earlier part of the eighth
century. Initial impoverishment in the early seventh century
was attributed to the Persian (Sasanid) occupation in 614 CE,
an explanation often proffered for many other church sites in
Israel (Tsafrir 1993: index 'Persian Conquest/Invasion'), but the
impact of which may well have been often exaggerated (Schick
1995: 20-48). Unfortunately, while many churches exhibited
clear evidence for continued use into Umayyad times, the focus
on churches meant that only one kind of evidence was recovered, and although atypical such evidence was frequently used
to compose generalised settlement histories, especially ones
that dwelt on the 'fate' of Christian communities in Islamic
times. In the end proposed site chronologies based on these
excavations turned out to be little different from those offered
thirty years earlier, but with the improvement in recording and
reporting standards the conclusions were more open to questioning and re-evaluation.

1. Defining Islamic archaeology in Syria-Palestine

At the beginning of the 1980s a seismic shift took place in attitude and practice in the archaeology of Islamic Syria-Palestine. Theoretical, methodological and practical approaches directly applicable to properly investigating social, cultural and economic conditions in Islamic times were adopted. The importance of investigating Islamic-period occupation as a clearly defined and independent research objective was recognised for both regional survey work and site excavation. While at first such developments could be somewhat ill-defined, for instance with Sydney University's work at Pella (in which I took part), by the end of the decade Islamic archaeology was firmly established as a discrete and recognisable field in its own right. In the Jordanian context this recognition found prominent expression in a series of papers dealing with issues of continuity delivered at the Fourth International Conference on the History and Archaeology of Jordan, held at Lyon between 30 May and 4 June 1989 (Johns 1992, 1994; Walmsley 1992; Whitcomb 1992). Feathers may have been ruffled, but a strong voice had been given to new ideas and new methods.

Over to the west, in Israel-Palestine, developments in the 1980s were not as rapid or apparent, but new approaches were nevertheless being applied by younger researchers, laying the foundation for a fresh reappraisal of rural settlement patterns in early Islamic times, especially in the south. Both regional survey work, undertaken as part of the Israel Antiquities Authority's 'Archaeological Survey of Israel', and focused small-scale excavations increasingly recognised widespread and, in some areas, expanding occupation in the arid Darum and Naqab/Negev region into Islamic times. Gideon Avni (1994, 1996), Mordechai Haiman (1995a, 1995b) and Yesha'yahu Lender (1990) in particular were receptive to new understandings of ceramic chronologies datable to the late antique/early Islamic transition, with their published survey results identifying considerable continuity of settlement, as

27

will be discussed in more detail in Chapter 3. These conclusions stood in stark contrast to earlier interpretations of a destructive Islamic conquest of the area's townships as proposed, for example, at Avdat/Oboda (Negev 1997: 9), or a retraction in settlement and abandonment by *c.* 700 along the lines of the urban devolution model argued for sites in Jordan (e.g. Rehovot/Ruhaybah, Tsafrir 1988; Tsafrir and Holum 1993).

The 1980s also witnessed a resurgence of archaeological activity focusing on the Islamic periods in Syria, although the 1960s and 1970s in Syria had not been as devoid of activity or as intellectually negative compared to the situation further south in Jordan and Israel/Palestine. For instance, between 1964 and 1972, Oleg Grabar undertook a thorough investigation of the expansive complex at Qasr al-Hayr al-Sharqi, involving a detailed structural survey and controlled excavations, followed up by an exemplary publication of the results (Grabar et al. 1978). Also of note was the return to the village sites of northwest Syria by Jean-Pierre Sodini and Georges Tate between 1976 and 1978, this time with the added benefit of targeted archaeological excavations. Their discoveries brought into question many of Tchalenko's earlier conclusions (Sodini et al. 1980; Tate 1992). Sodini and Tate argued that, rather than seventh-century abandonment, occupation on an extensive scale continued into the ninth century at least, and perhaps later. As the economy was considerably more diversified than the olive monoculture proposed by Tchalenko, its continued strength was not dependent on distant markets, especially those in Western Europe. The 1980s projects in Syria continued the advances seen in the work of the previous decade or two. Islamic archaeology had become characteristically systematic in intent, comprehensive in scope, mindful of earlier neglect (at least in some areas) with previous work and, moreover, set out to interpret the retrieved data within a broader social and economic context. Survey work, for instance in the

Balikh Valley in northeast Syria (Bartl 1994), and new excavations at major sites such as Madinat al-Far, Raqqah and
Rusafah, where a large mosque was uncovered next to the
cathedral in 1983-6 (Sack 1996), marked a fresh start for Islamic archaeology in Syria.

Overall, then, an increasingly identifiable branch of archaeology expressly concerned with the study of the cultural
heritage of the Islamic world was shaped out of the intellectual
melting pot of the 1980s, and has since grown into one of the
most dynamic areas of archaeological research in Syria-Palestine today. A new group of scholars has arisen, educated in
modern theoretical and methodological approaches in addition
to more conventional architecture and art history while being
cognisant, through grounding in historical studies, of the
strengths and weaknesses of written sources. In the last two
decades the advances in Syria-Palestine have been exciting and
palpable, resulting in the formation of a discipline that is
progressive, yet conscious of existing strengths, as I hope the
next chapters will demonstrate. No longer does Islamic archaeology simply provide a 'gap filler' service for historians, a
monologue-narrative in which established intellectual frameworks are augmented with interesting and curious details.
While Islamic archaeology continues to offer much new information relevant to the study of history, architecture and art
history, its goals have expanded into something much more
ambitious, becoming an independent arbitrator – for historical
sources were commonly written to an agenda with a point to
prove – and an elaborator, offering depth, complexity and completely new dimensions absent in historical sources, and often
challenging how they are to be understood. Archaeology produces a category of evidence that, when adequately interpreted,
is an unbiased first-hand record of things as they were, and
while the interpretation of the discoveries can be doubted the
raw data that spawned them can not be disputed. This role for

archaeology is not a new idea, but only in recent years have Islamic archaeologists, at least in Syria-Palestine, hungrily sought to identify such broader intellectual objectives.

Western scholarship dealing with the Islamic world has been accused of being stubbornly self-justifying, princely and mannish in character. The early archaeology of the Islamic world, including that in Syria-Palestine, reflected this bias, especially with its emphasis on monumental architecture and elite art objects analysed from a purely dynastic perspective. Other social groups such as women, children and minorities have been mostly invisible to scholarship, a failing common to all historical studies but given further validation in this case by male, Western, perceptions of Islam. Uniquely, archaeology offers new, reliable and almost unlimited data with which the social history of Islamic Syria-Palestine can be understood from a non-elitist and post-colonial perspective. In addition to fulfilling a traditional role of supporting and expanding the capabilities of earlier fields of study (although in new ways), archaeological research will also assist in greatly improving our understanding of formation processes in the lead up to modern Islamic society (see, recently, Whitcomb 2004), a contribution desperately needed given current tensions in the international environment. In this, the relevance and importance of Islamic archaeology is greater now than it has ever been, especially in the context of Syria-Palestine.

2

After Justinian, 565-635 CE

In the musings of many Western scholars, the two fateful generations following the death of the Byzantine emperor Justinian (r. 527-65) were characterised by widespread social and economic decline in Syria-Palestine, particularly in urban life. These ultimately terminal failures, commonly if somewhat loosely linked to short-sighted imperial policies adopted by Justinian's successors, exposed Syria-Palestine to the military reality of Sasanid assault and a subsequent 'conquest' – as unexpected as it was swift – by an emergent and energised Muslim political entity emanating out of the Hijaz area of the Arabian Peninsula (Fig. 1). At the risk of oversimplifying and, even worse, misrepresenting the views of other scholars – views that can change over the life of a scholar – the explanations for these events are worth summarising. The problem has been addressed from two perspectives in archaeology.

The first suggested cause was misguided military planning by the Byzantines, whose primary object in the east was containing Sasanid Persia. From the time of Justinian, it was argued, the protection of the Arabian border had been transferred to client Arab tribes, notably the Ghassanids, resulting in the withdrawal of standing forces from a line of defensive forts along the Arabian border, the grandly titled *limes arabicus* (recently, Parker 2000: 383-4; 2006: 562-71). This system apparently worked well for a while, but by the end of the sixth century had failed due to Byzantine negligence. As a consequence, the southeast reaches of the empire lay perilously

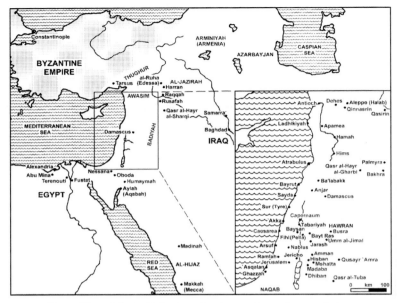

Fig. 1. Map of Syria-Palestine showing major regions and sites
(see also Fig. 7; Walmsley).

open and undefended – a view that has found wide acceptance
(e.g. Brown 1971: 170).

A second suggested cause for the swift capitulation of Syria-
Palestine identified socio-cultural factors, especially a
perceived decline in urban vitality as revealed in archaeological
data. This explanation argued that the defining features of the
classical town in Syria-Palestine, which were seen as im-
mensely successful, were steadily eroded during the second half
of the sixth century until they were but weak shadows of their
former grand selves. By the start of seventh century, the vitality of the Greek-inspired *polis* had been replaced by an
emancipated and socially narrow substitute, a fledgling
Arab/Muslim *madinah* (the classic and much-quoted study is
Kennedy 1985a). Syria-Palestine, it was thus argued, simply

32

did not have the wherewithal to resist a more powerful, and organised, intruder.

Several historians have addressed the issue of the inability, or unwillingness, of Syria-Palestine to resist the Sasanid and especially Muslim incursions from a different angle, but one that, in some ways, intersects with the urban decline model of archaeologists. Rather than concentrating on economic or military factors, some writers, Fred Donner (1981: 92-6) for instance, have tackled the question from an ethno-cultural viewpoint. To them, the failure of the inhabitants of Syria-Palestine to defy, even repel, outside assailants could be attributed to the persistence among the local population of a collective and entrenched Semitic mentality only superficially influenced by many years of Hellenistic culture, and a dislike, even hatred, of their Byzantine overlords with whom longstanding disagreements on the nature of Christ, itself a symptom of the cultural gulf between Hellene and Semite, had forged irreparable division (summarised, with bibliography, in Kennedy 1999: 226-7). For these reasons, it was argued, the east would hastily cast off, with no obvious regrets, more than a thousand years of Hellenistic culture. By no means unanimously accepted, for other writers have argued that the adoption of Hellenism and its translation into something distinctively local, indeed indigenous, is incontrovertible (Bowersock 1990: 71-82), this reasoning did seem to account for the apparent ease with which the Arab-Muslim armies were able to seize and hold Syria-Palestine from the Byzantines.

While the Islamic expansion was only part of a much longer process of an emerging Arab presence in Syria-Palestine that had began centuries before, it marked a clear and significant turning point in the history of the region that was not to reach a clearer definition until centuries later. For scholarship, the event has understandably always been central to comprehending the beginnings of Islam in the region, but remains, nonetheless, elusive to explanation. The situation is no different in archaeology. In recent years much research has been devoted to understanding the few decades leading up to the Islamic expansion into Syria-Palestine, partly to illuminate conditions before that momentous event and, perhaps, partly to offer explanations for the speed and success of the expansion. Interest in this period has also developed as part of a renewal of interest in early Byzantine studies and the condition of the Early Church in Syria-Palestine, and in the role and influence of pre-Islamic Arab groups in the region, about which the literature is extensive and increasing exponentially. This chapter looks at some of the critical issues in these fields from the perspective of recent archaeological discoveries, but also takes into account current historical research on the topics, and reviews what insights this work gives into understanding cultural and economic conditions in the towns and countryside of Syria-Palestine just before the Islamic expansion of the 630s.

The condition of towns in the later sixth century

Did towns decline after Justinian? Recent archaeology has much to contribute to a consideration of the matter with, overall, no uniform explanation that holds for all places. The picture is complex, but revealing.

In evaluating the urban history of the late antique east, the age of Justinian has always been viewed as some kind of 'Indian summer' closing out a long period of urban excellence in Syria-Palestine. In the eyes of many authors, much of the first half of the sixth century was characterised by urban renewal and extensive church building, and to some extent that is true (but, in retrospect, somewhat over emphasised in Walmsley 1996). The case can be argued especially for the major towns, such as Antioch, Apamea, Jerusalem, Caesarea Maritima (Holum and

Hohlfelder 1988: 175-6) and Scythopolis (Tsafrir and Foerster 1997: 116-17). At Antioch, the city was rebuilt after an earthquake in 528 and, later, streets and public buildings were reconstructed in line with earlier conventions following the Sasanid devastations in 541. Likewise at Apamea, considerable resources were put into rebuilding the town following destructive earthquakes in the 520s (Kennedy and Liebeschuetz 1989: 65-7). In Jerusalem, new streets were built to link Justinian's grand *Nea* church, dedicated in 543, with the city's crowning glory, the *Martyrium* church of Constantine (307-37) at the site of Christ's crucifixion and burial. Excavations reveal that Justinian's cardo was utterly conventional in its construction: a paved road twelve metres wide with shops fronted by five-metre deep porticoes. To the east a second cardo ran between the northern Neapolis (Damascus) gate and the Siloam church, this being also a twelve-metre wide paved and sewered street flanked by an arcaded colonnade, three-metre wide footways and shops (Geva 1993: 774-7, 779). The Justinianic streets constituted the final stage in a three-century evolution of the Byzantine city, a pictorial representation of which is preserved in a famous church mosaic of the late sixth or early seventh century at Madaba, Jordan (Donner and Cüppers 1977). Visually, emphasis is directed towards the gates, walls, streets and churches of Jerusalem – a precise summation of the important features of late antique towns in Palestine and Arabia. Other towns also received attention in the first half of the sixth century, largely due to initiatives by the local population. Living quarters were rebuilt, for instance to a grid at Pella (Watson 1992: 163-70), water systems repaired or improved, and walls erected, as at Tiberias (Hirschfeld 1999: 238-40), not so much for defensive reasons but as a mark of civic status, as the mosaic depictions of towns have shown.

The first half of the sixth century was a period of widespread church building in Syria-Palestine, especially Palestine, because of its religious associations (Patrich 1995: 477-9). Many of the churches uncovered so far have been attributed to the time of Justinian I, although sometimes more for convenience than for good reason. At Jarash/Gerasa for instance, where some fifteen churches have been identified within the town limits, construction apparently peaked in the second quarter of the sixth century (Sartre 1985: 136-8). However, at least one of the churches at first attributed to the time of Justinian, that dedicated to SS Peter and Paul in the western part of the town, is almost certainly later in date, probably early seventh century (Gatier 1987: 135), but perhaps even later. Another case of civic misdating, this time from Scythopolis (Baysan), illustrates how serious the problem of misattribution can be. A rebuilt street, lined with an impressive complex of shops, was initially dated to the early sixth century; only after the discovery of a Kufic inscription was the correct, Umayyad, date acknowledged (Tsafrir and Foerster 1997: 118). These examples demonstrate the fundamental flaw in making attributions based solely on stylistic comparisons or, worse, simply on an assumption. Building activity in the early sixth century has been seriously inflated as a result, while subsequent periods are doubtless underrepresented.

In part, if not predominantly, as a result of errors in dating the constructional histories of sites, urban activity in Syria-Palestine after Justinian has been conventionally interpreted as a time of significant decline (Kennedy 1985b: esp. 150-1). Arguments are commonly based on epigraphic evidence, especially the lack of building inscriptions for the second half of the sixth century, such as at Scythopolis (Tsafrir and Foerster 1997: 118, 125-6, 140-3). Frequently cited causes are repeated occurrences of the plague, including a severe outbreak in 558 followed by another in 573-4, often associated with famine (Stathakopoulos 2004), recurring earthquakes (Guidoboni, Comastri and Traina 1994), Persian incursions in 540 and 573, revolts by ethnoreligious groups such as the Samaritans in 529, and environmental factors (Kennedy 1985b: 181-3). While the cumulative effects of all these factors may have acted negatively on some centres at different times, notably Antioch and perhaps Apamea, it is quite possible that their overall impact on urban life in the second half of the sixth century has been exaggerated. The problem is interpretative rather than factual: the absence of engraved inscriptions does not necessarily indicate a lack of economic activity; urban developments that do not meet Western concepts of a 'proper' classical city have been dismissed as evidence for decline; while the chronology of material culture after the mid-sixth century is still poorly defined, especially for ceramics. Archaeology is only just beginning to offer new interpretations of site histories that demonstrate greater continuity, but continuity that allows for change, and a flatter pattern of civic and economic activity throughout the sixth century. There is plenty of evidence for a strong settlement profile for Syria-Palestine after Justinian, and not only in towns. Recent work also demonstrates convincingly that rural areas around the towns underwent a settlement expansion in the later sixth and early seventh centuries, thereby creating a new urban-rural dynamic that perhaps favoured the countryside over towns. These issues, which were to redefine the purpose and function of towns and the countryside in Syria-Palestine during the decades leading up to the Islamic expansion, are the focus of the rest of this chapter.

Much has been written on the question of structural change in the planning and organisation of urban thoroughfares after antiquity in Syria-Palestine. As we saw in Chapter 1, in the 1930s and 1940s the French scholar Jean Sauvaget argued that the alteration from broad colonnaded streets to narrow covered markets, or *suq*, was a common feature of towns in the Islamic middle ages, based on his examination of Ladhikiyah (Latakia) and Aleppo. This view was widely accepted until the publication

in the mid-1980s of Hugh Kennedy's influential study of change
in the cities of late antiquity, entitled 'From *polis* to *madina*'
(Kennedy 1985a). In that article, which has now become a
standard reference on the topic, Kennedy argues coherently
and with conviction that the ultimately irrevocable constriction
of streets with shops and houses began, not in Islamic times,
but in the last decades of Byzantine rule in Syria-Palestine,
finally putting to an end the role of the Hellenistic agora as the
primary commercial hub of the city. To Kennedy, it represented
the beginning of a process that carried on deep into Islamic
times (Kennedy 1985a: 11-13). The evidence offered in support
of his thesis was predominantly archaeological, drawn from
excavation results at Jarash, Apamea and Antioch.

A major problem with Kennedy's reference material was its
chronological weakness; for Antioch, for instance, his argument
was based on the assumption that an absence of deposits over
the street paving indicated a short chronological period between street and encroachment (Kennedy 1985a: 12; 1985b:
153). Work since the appearance of Kennedy's articles does
confirm that urban augmentation became increasingly common
from the mid-sixth century onwards, but also shows that, contrary to Kennedy's view, this was clearly no haphazard or
random event that assaulted classical elegance through its
chaotic demeanour. As yet unpublished thesis work on Jarash
by Ian Simpson, in which he combines archival material with
the results of new excavations, shows that the structures built
along the south cardo, the south decumanus, on the oval piazza
and over the plaza around the south tetrakionia were accommodated carefully and sympathetically within the existing urban
plan (see further below, Chapter 4 and Fig. 9). Commercial
units, some devoted to light industrial purposes, were extended
over built-up sidewalks up to and, in places, beyond the street
colonnades, but the paved central part of the streets remained
open and functional as thoroughfares. Piped water ran the

length of the cardo, feeding water basins placed periodically along the street, and continued into the centre of the oval piazza, terminating at a large basin that supplied water to a new quarter, again added sympathetically to the existing plan. There is nothing especially disorderly in all of this; rather the evidence argues for a planned expansion of commercial activity in central Jarash, perhaps organised by civic authorities who also benefited from making redundant public space available for commercial enterprise. While dating is still problematic, the discovery of a coin hoard of the early seventh century under floor levels in the oval piazza would suggest that these changes were instituted, although not completed (as will be seen below), at Jarash over the later sixth and early seventh centuries.

The question is: do these structural modifications reflect broader socio-economic changes? Do we see in these developments the beginnings of an urban merchant group of manufacturers and traders that came to typify town economies of the Islamic middle ages? The expansion of markets into the bustling, busy places that must have impressed any visitor was probably related to the growth of industrial activity in towns at the same time, as these activities became common in many towns in early Islamic Syria-Palestine (see below, Chapter 4). Hence the *polis* had begun to transform into a *madinah* before Islam, but carefully and in an orderly manner, and socially as well as structurally.

Further evidence for continued economic activity opposed to decline in the later sixth and early seventh centuries is contained in two quite different categories of data: one numismatic, the other archaeological. Both shed considerable light on what can be a difficult period to identify, and both contradict the idea of a major collapse in economic conditions after Justinian.

A study of nearly 300 copper coins found during excavations at Pella and Jarash demonstrates that the supply of coinage reached a noticeable peak during the reign of Justin II (565-78)

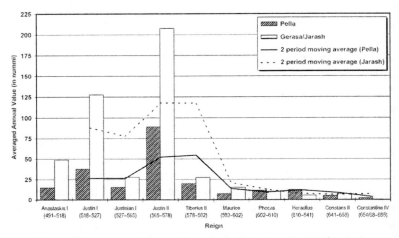

Fig. 2. Coinage supply in southern Syria-Palestine during the sixth
to early seventh century (Walmsley).

and, perhaps contrary to expectations, not during that of his
predecessor Justinian I (Fig. 2, Walmsley 1999). Given the
predominance of three central mints, Constantinople, Nikome-
dia and Thessalonica (the latter only at Jarash), the increased
supply under Justin II can be attributed to a major rise in
official consignments, most probably as military pay to counteract the Sasanid incursion of 573 that culminated in the sack of
Apamea. After Tiberius II (578-82), in whose reign annual
supply surprisingly matched that of Justinian, coin numbers
fell back to levels representative of local circulation, not special
payments. Supply at Pella, however, was an exception: a perceptible rise occurred in the time of Phocas (602-10) and
Heraclius (610-41), which probably reflected a greater military
presence there during the time of the Heraclii revolt and the
Sasanid threat. Archaeological work at Pella confirms this
suggestion, as revealed in the sizeable expansion of a hill-top
garrison to house a large detachment of cavalry at about this
time. Together, the coin data would suggest that the region

40

south of Damascus did have a military role to play in the last quarter of the sixth and the first quarter of the seventh century, counteracting to some extent the idea of an enfeebled and undefended south. The ongoing presence of a garrison at Pella, strategically located midway between Damascus and Jerusalem, was probably the reason for an otherwise inexplicable major encounter there in 635 between Muslim and Byzantine forces.

Other evidence for a pronounced level of economic activity in Syria-Palestine after Justinian has, in recent years, resulted from exploratory survey work and excavations in the environmentally marginal areas of the region, especially the Negev and the Jordanian steppe lands east of Amman, otherwise known as the *badiyah*. The surviving architecture at sites such as Umm al-Jimal, Rihab, Khirbat al-Samra and Umm al-Rasas is testament to the expansion of rural settlement in the later sixth and early seventh centuries. These seemingly rambling sites, each 'unclassical' in plan, feature many churches, often decorated with mosaics that include a dated, dedicatory inscription. An important study by Leah Di Segni (1999; see also Walmsley 2005) has shown that a substantial leap in building activity took place in the badiyah villages of Jordan during the reigns of Maurice, Phocas and Heraclius, peaking in the reign of Phocas. While dated monuments are increasingly rare in towns, 'villages flourish: at least, this is evident in the eastern part of [Jordan]. The first dated church at Rihab was founded in 533 and renovated in 583; then new churches sprout like mushrooms after a rainstorm, 8 of them between 594 and 635 – in 594, 595, 605, 620, 623 (2 churches), and 635 (2 churches)' (Di Segni 1999: 165). A similar pattern of extensive church building is observable at Khirbat al-Samra and Umm al-Rasas. Samra gained eight churches, three with dated mosaics of 633/35, 634 and 637, notably right in the midst of the Islamic expansion through the area. There can be no clearer evidence

41

not only for widespread economic prosperity, but also for an emergent strategic role for the *badiyah* as Arab-Christian tribes, such as the Ghassanids, found new and tangible ways to express an emergent socio-political role in their relations with a transforming Byzantine polity (Shahîd 1995; 2002). Other factors for the foundation of permanent settlements may have been climatic amelioration, land degradation and flight from cities in fear of the plague and earthquakes, but the evidence – mostly deduced from later written sources – has a tendency to be vague and overly determinist.

The plans of these steppe settlements differ from those of the towns in agricultural areas in that they do not exhibit an apparent order based on eastern classical precedents. There are no columned streets or symmetrical plazas draped neatly around an urban grid; the organisation of sites appears quite random, almost 'spontaneous'. This is, however, a strange way to view these settlements, because why should they follow such a predetermined order? In fact, from the overall site plan down to individual dwellings, another order is at work, for these settlements are not without a common structure in the midst of apparent chaos – a chaos made worse by modifications ancient and modern and the visual state of the ruins when first encountered. Umm al-Jimal in northeast Jordan is one of the clearer examples (Fig. 3, Knauf 1984; de Vries 1998, 2000). Activity at Umm al-Jimal, a Christian Arab settlement, was particularly high in the sixth and seventh centuries, during which the preserved plan of the site was finalised. The layout consisted of three groups of building clusters, each cluster usually facing out onto common ground. Large areas of open space separated each cluster group, although as this space was partitioned by walls it was still owned and utilised, probably at the community level. Each cluster consisted of a variable number of building units, between six and 24, with some units co-joined to form a block, commonly of three to five units. Some clusters had their own

42

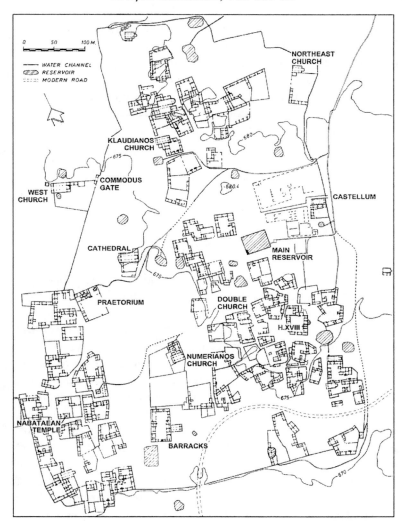

Fig. 3. Plan of Umm al-Jimal in north Jordan
(after de Vries 1998: 94).

integrated church, some not; three other large churches, perhaps one for each grouping, stood outside the cluster arrangement to serve the whole community, perhaps not just the residents of Umm al-Jimal. Each house unit, usually double- or triple-storeyed, conformed to a standard plan made up of conjoined rooms around an enclosed, private courtyard. Hence a clear settlement hierarchy and thus social structure is apparent:

group – cluster – block – unit, enforcing a progressive social
    transition between:
public – privileged – restricted – private, originating in a social
    structure of:
community – tribe – clan – extended family.

This structure reflects tribal norms prevalent in Arab society in the pre-Islamic period, also vividly encapsulated in the classical poetry of the period (Fahd 1997).

Even noting the various cautions that must be kept in mind when setting out to visualise late antique towns in Syria-Palestine, when we come to consider urban life on the eve of the Islamic expansion it must be remembered that these towns had changed irrevocably compared with their classical predecessors, a fact not always appreciated when visiting the visually 'sanitised' tourist sites these places have been turned into today. Commerce and trade was an increasingly important facet of urban life, revealed in the growing size and density of markets. Socially, towns were also in transition. By the end of the sixth century the Church and the extended family had become the main focus of urban life, regulated by a bishop and patriarchal head respectively, these being synonymous in role and only differentiated in social scale. Parallels in Islamic social practices are apparent. Archaeologically, this distinctly late antique social structure finds expression in the organisation of towns and villages in Syria-Palestine, as seen at Umm al-Jimal and similar sites. Minorities, such as the Jews, were similarly organised, as the many Galilean synagogues and associated villages attest (Foerster 1992). However, none of this denotes weakness; rather, it suggests flexibility in an age of rapid and considerable social and economic change. In this light the towns of Syria-Palestine appear well prepared for the challenges of the seventh century.

The impact of multiple conquests

> For some scholars, the 'Islamic Conquest' of Syria is still an unexplainable catastrophe which flooded a flourishing country with hordes of barbarian Bedouin and vandals, destroying an old culture and cutting it off from the rest of the world, by which they mean from Western Europe. It is hard to imagine a view which is more aberrant (Knauf 1987: 77).

The churches of the Jordanian *badiyah* described above, especially those at Samra, demonstrate that neither the Sasanid conquest nor the Islamic expansion had any perceptible impact thereabouts. Churches were being built at the very moment the Muslim armies were passing through the area towards Damascus, and all of these churches show no evidence whatsoever that they suffered any appreciable damage or were destroyed. Similarly elusive in the archaeological record is the earlier Sasanid occupation of 613-28, even if later Christian sources accuse the conquerors of extensive atrocities. Based on these blindingly vitriolic written accounts, archaeologists have habitually credited perceived church destructions to the Sasanid advance (see above), but many of these attributions are not at all certain chronologically or archaeologically, while some were possibly the result of a period of anarchy following the Sasanid conquest

(Schick 1989: 20-48). However, even the supposed evidence for widespread destruction in Jerusalem with the Sasanid occupation can be questioned, for instance with the *Nea* church of Justinian. Overall, while churches in some towns may have been damaged during or after the Sasanid conquest, the infrastructure of towns suffered little from the arrival of the Sasanids; the projected 540 and 573 urban devastations of Antioch and Apamea respectively were not repeated on a wider scale.

For the inhabitants of Syria-Palestine the passage of armies was never to be taken lightly, and the situation in the early seventh century was in no way different. The perceived dangers of an approaching army at the level of individuals is rarely recorded and hard to guess, but the recovery of a number of coin hoards datable to the 610s to 630s gives a poignant insight into the real threat posed by an advancing army and the strong fear it could generate. Of eighteen early seventh-century hoards of gold and copper coin in Syria-Palestine, fifteen can be attributed to the Sasanid threat based on the last dated coin in each hoard, usually anywhere between 602 and 612. Only three hoards included a coin late enough to attribute it to the Muslim advance. At first glance, for it must be admitted that establishing when a hoard was concealed can be difficult, the higher number of hoards attributable to the Sasanid incursion may indicate that the 610s were a time of considerable insecurity for individuals, especially following the capture of Antioch (Walmsley 2000: 269). Painful memories of events in the previous century, when the Sasanids extorted large amounts of cash from towns like Apamea, impelled individuals to bury their wealth, but interestingly many of these hoards were not recovered with the eventual eviction of the Sasanid forces in 628. It appears as though owners were reluctant to recover their wealth while conditions remained insecure after 613-14, during which time they may have died, moved or forgotten the exact location of the hoard. Overall, then, the coin evidence shows that the Sasanid offensive in Syria-Palestine resulted in real financial loss for individuals and the community alike, and it would be mistaken to dismiss as insignificant the negative social and economic impact of over a decade of Sasanid occupation.

By way of contrast, the arrival of Muslim forces into Syria-Palestine from the Arabian Peninsula in 634 and the subsequent taking of the whole region between 635 and 640 are so indiscernible in the archaeological record that this historically momentous sequence of events has been appropriately termed the 'Invisible Conquest' (Pentz 1992). The supposed evidence for destructive incursions into the Negev by 'Arabs' has been overwhelmingly refuted in a recent publication by Jodi Magness (2003: 177-94). Major urban sites similarly show a complete absence of damage. The extensive excavation of important centres at the time of the Islamic expansion, such as Baysan, Pella, Jarash, Bayt Ras, Amman and Apamea has failed to turn up one shred of evidence in favour of destruction to churches, houses and civic utilities (Lenzen and Knauf 1987: 37-9; MacAdam 1986; Tsafrir and Foerster 1997: 144; Walmsley 1988). Sources record that most cities capitulated without a fight, with Caesarea and Asqalan/Ascalon being two exceptions. Each city, usually represented by its bishop, entered into a treaty with the Muslim leader in which religious and personal rights were guaranteed. Even Caesarea, although taken by force, failed to produce any definite evidence for urban devastation in the archaeological record (Holum 1992). Led by its cities, Syria-Palestine passed quietly and almost willingly without even the slightest whimper into a new and momentous age, the significance of which was neither recognised nor appreciated at the time.

Material culture and society

As was argued in the previous chapter, the expansion of Islam into Syria-Palestine in the 630s was accompanied by only minimal disruption to socio-economic life in both towns and the countryside, and no more congruent argument exists for a predominantly smooth transition from Byzantine to Islamic times than that deduced from the evidence preserved in the material culture of the age. For almost two generations after the Islamic expansion the objects that were produced, traded and used in Syria-Palestine displayed very little variation from those in use in the decades before the arrival of Islam. Indeed, the seventh century stands out as one of the more conservative periods in the cultural record of late antique and early Islamic Syria-Palestine. Changes in a whole range of artefact classes – pottery, glass and coins for instance – show almost imperceptible developments over three generations. Most of the seventh century comes across as a time of considerable monotony, in which cultural traditions responded only slowly to a new, emergent, political reality.

As is often the case in archaeology, such a lack of definition in the material culture record has been one of the biggest problems in correctly identifying and explaining societal change in the seventh century. Until recently it has been very much a 'hidden century', both archaeologically and architecturally (Johns 2003). This cultural lacuna has posed particular problems in survey work and excavations. The full occupational range of sites has not been recognised, thereby creating incomplete settlement profiles. The analysis of these results, when attempted, has led to serious misunderstanding and error, as will be investigated in the following chapter. Fortunately, recent work has done much to recover this 'lost' century from oblivion through the proper identification of a clearly identifiable material cultural horizon for the period, especially in ceramics and, of late, glass and coins.

By comparison the cultural setting of the eighth and ninth centuries is much better understood due to the appearance – and preservation – of monumental architecture, more extensive archaeological discoveries at sites and, unlike the seventh century, very rapid change in all classes of material culture (for an excellent introduction, see Museum with No Frontiers 2000). Thus there are not as many problems in identifying eighth- and, generally, ninth-century cultural developments; the major difficulties still remaining are, first, the patchy coverage of knowledge, for some geographical areas and time periods are still only scantily understood, and secondly, how the different changes in these centuries can be understood and explained. This chapter reviews these developments and points out the problems that remain; their implications for building settlement profiles and understanding the economy are considered in the chapters that follow.

Pottery and early Islamic society

The study of pottery remains a cornerstone of Middle Eastern archaeology, but the modern study of ceramics goes well beyond the narrow antiquarian or chronological objectives of the past. The thorough collection and systematic processing of pottery during survey work and excavations permit the application of advanced analytical techniques, and can help to trace wider trends within an ancient society by identifying stylistic and technological changes to the corpus. However, such analyses

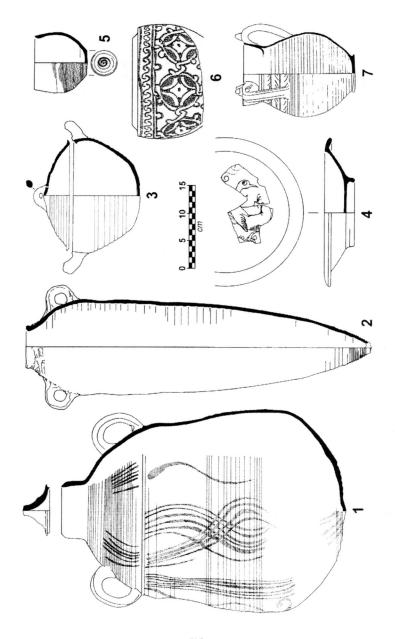

50

are valid only if the chronological foundations are secure. Islamic archaeology in Syria-Palestine over the last 30 years has managed to make great strides in both areas of research.

As in earlier periods, the ceramics of early Islamic Syria-Palestine can be classified into five broad groupings, and in keeping with the low cultural impact of the political events of the early seventh century the ceramics of the first Islamic decades show little diversion from those current immediately before (there is no space here for detailed descriptions: see especially Sauer and Magness 1997; Schick 1998; Sodini and Villeneuve 1992; Walmsley 1995; Whitcomb 1988b). These five categories are: containers, cooking vessels, serving wares, domestic utilitarian objects such as lamps and lanterns, and building materials, specifically roof, wall and floor tiles.

Containers were a major category, used for storage and transport of foodstuffs and liquids. Ubiquitous in the archaeological record are large, brittle thin-walled jars for the collection of water (in Arabic, a *zir*) often decorated with white-painted 'double helix' patterns (Fig. 4.1). Water was stored in thicker-walled, porous white-ware jars, which served to cool water by gradual evaporation from the outside surface of the vessel. Amphorae, thick-walled vessels used for the long-distance transport of major commodities, especially olive oil and wine, are an interesting class of pottery as the survival of these vessels in the archaeological record offers a firm indicator of interregional trade, as considered in Chapter 5. The major amphora types in south Syria-Palestine during early Islamic times originated from Gaza (Fig. 4.2), Aqabah, Abu Mina and Terenouti, the last two located in the western delta of Egypt.

Fig. 4. A selection of diagnostic early Islamic pottery from southern Syria-Palestine. 1-2: storage jars, mid-seventh to eighth century; 3: cooking bowl (casserole), eighth century: 4: Jerash bowl, seventh century; 5: Palestinian Fine ware, eighth-ninth century; Red Painted bowl in mosaic pattern (Palace ware), eighth-ninth century; 7: Cream ware (Mafjar ware), later eighth to tenth century (Pella Excavations/University of Sydney).

Equally common were vessels used for cooking food, mostly open jars and casseroles with lids made from a gritty, shock-resistant ware (Fig. 4.3). These vessels were locally produced in great numbers, with kilns at, for instance, Jarash and Baysan. Specimens often retain evidence of use in the excessive blackening of their bases. Their very utilitarian nature means that stylistic change in the container and cooking categories of ceramics occurred only slowly over time, making them poor chronological indicators.

Fortunately, serving wares provide a major diagnostic group in the ceramics of early Islamic Syria-Palestine, as these were intended for display and hence were the most decorated ware by the use of paint, incision, and appliqué. Glazed wares, in Syria-Palestine generally not introduced until the later eighth century at the earliest, always represented a small minority in the ceramic assemblage throughout the early Islamic period. Serving vessels included plates, platters, bowls, cups and small jugs and juglets. In the seventh and perhaps early eighth century some types of fine-ware plates were brought in from Egypt and Cyprus in the final phase of a Mediterranean-wide exchange in Late Roman wares (Hayes 1972, 1980). The discontinuation of this trade, probably fall-out from the ending of state-subsidised wheat shipments to Constantinople under Heraclius, encouraged further the local production of decorated plates and dishes, including the magnificently produced Jarash Bowls and large red-painted platters (Fig. 4.4; Uscatescu 1996; Watson 1989). Another important type of pottery is a series of cups, bowls, jars and jugs in a very thin pale orange to light reddish-brown fabric, perhaps intended to imitate prestige metallic vessels in gold (Fig. 4.5). Known originally as 'Fine Byzantine ware', this ware type first appeared in the sixth century and continued strongly into the ninth century and probably later, and hence is more early Islamic than Byzantine. Distribution studies suggest the pottery type was made in the

Jerusalem area, and would be better called Palestinian Fine ware to avoid chronological confusion (see the important studies in Magness 1993: 166-71; Sauer and Magness 1997: 476). Decoration of the outside surfaces featured knife burnishing, an incised wavy line on cups and, in the sixth and seventh centuries, cut strokes on jars and jugs. In the early eighth century dishes and plates appeared, perhaps in place of the increasingly unavailable Late Roman fine wares, to which paint was sometimes added, while the cups became more elongated, thinner-walled and round-based, approaching (as much as clay allows) the fineness of contemporary glass beakers but in elegance probably imitating metal prototypes. The parallel development in a hard, well-fired ware decorated in free-flowing abstract designs of swirls, asterisks and wavy lines in deep red to dark reddish-brown paint offers a comparable perspective on early Islamic ceramics in Syria-Palestine. Produced in the Amman area and at Jarash, Red Painted ware first appeared in the earlier part (second quarter?) of the eighth century in the shape of jars and jugs, but around the middle of the century the repertoire was expanded to include cups, bowls and platters. The bowls, known as 'palace ware' (Fig. 4.6), were probably used as tableware, for they rank as outstanding examples of the potters' art, both technically and artistically. The bowls, high-walled with an elegantly finished lip to the rim, were commonly slipped on the outside with a whitish wash, over which was applied an elaborate decorative regime of painted linear and stylised floral motifs, clearly inspired by mosaic patterns. It can be no coincidence that the mosaic-inspired decoration of the Red Painted bowls developed towards the end of the Umayyad period, at which time the mosaicist's art reached a high point with commissions at Khirbat Mafjar with the floor of the grand reception hall of Walid II (740s).

All the above wares grew out of, or were based on, existing ceramic and ornamental traditions in Syria-Palestine at the time of the Islamic expansion, but towards the end of the eighth or early in the ninth century ceramic tastes underwent a sudden and significant transformation, a process recognisable a cultural 'punctuation point' due to the decisiveness of the stylistic changes involved. In the material cultural record, this punctuation point was identifiable by the widespread adoption of new and exotic pottery types inspired by developments outside of the region, notably the introduction of brightly glazed wares (for these see Northedge 2001) and a range of elaborate jars and jugs in a thin, pale cream ware (Fig. 4.7). This latter ceramic type, almost certainly imitating silver vessels, originated in eighth-century Iraq and became a common domestic ware in Samarra, the Abbasid capital for much of the ninth century. The hint, no matter how distant, of wealth and a luxurious lifestyle inherent in these vessels guaranteed the rapid spread of the type throughout Syria-Palestine. Manufactured by fast wheel and in moulds at major centres such as Raqqah, Ramlah and Tabariyah, Cream ware vessels were in stark contrast with what had gone before. They were characterised by sharp, elbow-like angular profiles inspired by metal prototypes and extensively decorated with incised, applied and moulded patterns, as represented in the extensive corpus retrieved from excavations at Khirbat Mafjar, Caesarea, Capernaum and Pella, for instance (Magness 1997; Walmsley 2001; Whitcomb 1988b).

The persistent misdating of Palestinian Fine ware, Red Painted ware and Cream ware has hindered an appropriate appreciation of socio-economic developments in early Islamic Syria-Palestine. While the original study on Palestinian Fine ware recognised some continuity into Islamic times (Gichon 1974), the use of 'Byzantine' in the name and the failure to identify continuity after the middle of the eighth century disguised its predominantly Islamic attribution. Similarly, Red ware in all its forms was clumped together as one type into the

Umayyad period, thereby failing adequately to acknowledge a date chiefly in the period after (mid-eighth to ninth century). Even more misleading has been practise, especially in Israel, of dating all Cream wares (also known as 'Mefjar ware' after its early discovery at the Umayyad palace of Khirbat Mafjar near Jericho) solely to the Umayyad period, most conspicuously at Capernaum (Tzaferis 1989) and Caesarea (Levine and Netzer 1986). The error seemingly resulted from a misunderstanding of the chronology at Mafjar, compounded by misleading results from early excavations at Ramlah. Exposed basal levels, initially understood to be Umayyad but now recognised as Abbasid, produced examples of Cream ware, including moulds used in manufacturing, all of which was wrongly assigned an Umayyad date (refuted in Magness 1997; Walmsley 2001). The compression of important diagnostic ceramic groups into earlier periods, and especially the failure to recognise post-Umayyad sequences, has had a deleterious and long-lasting impact on accurately understanding the social history of early Islamic Syria-Palestine from an archaeological perspective. Because of these chronological errors, the Abbasid and Fatimid periods have been almost entirely written out of the archaeology of southern Syria-Palestine, thereby creating a false 'dark age' that has been difficult to dispel and replace with a more considered evaluation of socio-economic developments after the mid-eighth century.

All the major cultural trends outlined above – unbroken continuity from the Byzantine period, early eighth-century rejuvenation, and a late eighth- to early ninth-century innovation – are detailed in the Byzantine to early Islamic ceramic sequence recovered from the excavations at Pella, where a series of recognisable earthquake events have, with stratigraphical controls and tight coin dating, provided a secure ceramic chronology spanning the whole period from the sixth to tenth centuries (Walmsley 1995, 1997; Watson 1992). The excava-

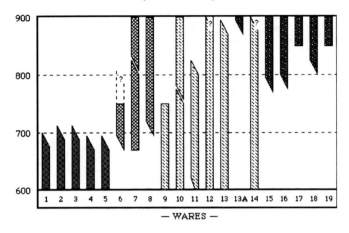

Fig. 5. Ware types and chronology of early Islamic pottery at Pella. Ware 1: Late Roman wares; Ware 2: 'Jerash Bowls'; Ware 3: Buff; Ware 4: Chaff-Tempered Coarse ware; Ware 5: Gaza amphora; Ware 6: Terenouti amphora; Ware 7: Pale Cream; Ware 8: Red Painted on light buff; Ware 9: Biscuit; Ware 10: Hard Fine terracotta; Ware 11: White Paint on Metallic terracotta; Ware 12: Brown Slipped White-painted (*zir*); Ware 13: Coarse terracotta (cooking ware); Ware 14: Dark Grey; Ware 15: Turquoise Glazed; Ware 16: Incised Polychrome Glazed; Ware 17: Yellow-Green Glazed; Ware 18: Incised Cream ('Mafjar') ware; Ware 19: Cut, Incised and Painted or 'Kerbschnitt' ware (Walmsley).

tions, supervised by the author in the 1980s (on which see further below, Chapter 5), concentrated on two areas: a comfortably equipped domestic quarter, where the extensive ruins of two-storeyed houses were exposed, and a new Islamic-period town centre built following a massive earthquake in the mid-eighth century. Current research has identified nineteen major wares in the Pella ceramic corpus between an earlier documented earthquake in 659-60 and the end of the Islamic city centre sometime in the tenth or eleventh century, although not all of these co-existed (Fig. 5). Reflected in the pottery corpus are some informative cultural trends in Syria-Palestine during early Islamic times. Major dynastic events, notably the arrival of Islam and the overthrow of the Umayyad Caliphs (750) had no appreciable impact on the ceramics, again illustrating the major error of equating pottery types with dynastic periods. Not until a few decades following the appearance of Islam, after a new ruling group was firmly in control, did perceptible shifts occur in the wares, shapes and technology represented in the pottery. At the start of the eighth century, five wares were no longer represented in the corpus (wares 1-5), while three new ones appeared (wares 6-8). These developments, however, did not alter the essentially local character of the corpus. The pottery of the eighth century clearly originated in the technologies of the preceding periods, with the changes representing local developments, not a radical break influenced by outside developments. The changes roughly coincided with the wide-ranging cultural and economic reforms initiated by the Umayyad caliph Abd al-Malik (685-705), and suggest social realignments sponsored by these reforms. Nevertheless, significant change in the ceramic repertoire was to come, but not until the end of the eighth or beginning of the ninth century, some two centuries after the imposition of Islamic hegemony. The extent of the change can be seen in the sudden end of the ubiquitous ware 11 made at Jarash and its replacement with the thin-walled, Samarra-style pale cream jars and strainer jugs of ware 18. This ware soon came to dominate the ceramic corpus of ninth-century Pella. Another change to traditional fabrics is noted with ware 13, where the dark brown cooking vessels were replaced by button-lidded casseroles in a more reddish fabric (ware 13A). The new type appears to be a precursor of the internally glazed Fatimid-period casseroles known from Amman citadel and other sites. Other previously unknown wares appear by the middle of the century, including Kerbschnitt bowls (ware 19) and occasional examples of glazed wares manufactued in the region but imitating Iraqi or Egyptian varieties (wares 15-17). The new pottery types, especially the cream jars and jugs and glazed wares, represent a profound artistic and technological break with the past. Traditional styles of pottery were abandoned in favour of external forms, bringing about an 'external revolution' that marked the start of a new phase in the Islamic ceramics of south Syria-Palestine. The adoption of cream and glazed wares at Pella suggests growing community involvement in the cultural traditions of a wider Islamic World – an interest that may represent the search for new, alternative identities following the decisive end by earthquake of late antique Pella and its institutions. The Pella ceramics are not the only example of this phenomenon; in north Syria, a similar broadening of ceramic traditions in Islamic times has been observed in the assemblage from Dehes/Dayhis (Orssaud 1992: 227).

Another equally significant change in ceramic traditions occurred in the eleventh century when local hand-made coarse pottery first appeared. Standing somewhat beyond the end of the chronological period covered in this book, the introduction of hand-made pottery was the beginnings of a new, village-produced pottery type that came to dominate the ceramic repertoire of the Islamic middle ages in Syria-Palestine (Johns 1998), and represented the next significant break with the past.

One final issue needs to be discussed before we move on from the ceramic traditions of early Islamic Syria-Palestine, and that is the widespread prevalence of divergent regional pottery traditions in the period. This issue is significant, as the growing incidence of regional styles after late antiquity, while beginning in that period, has further obfuscated accurate ceramic chronologies and, hence, skewed settlement profiles. While the pottery profiles of some areas for shorter and longer periods are well understood – north Jordan between the sixth and tenth centuries for example (above) – other places and times are poorly known (Sodini and Villeneuve 1992: 211). Many of the dating problems for south Jordan and the Negev can be directly attributed to an inadequate knowledge of ceramics (for the Negev, Magness 2003: esp. 7). Relatively recent work at Gharandal and Humaymah has begun to produce a corpus of early Islamic wares for south Jordan that are remarkable for their stark dissimilarity to northern Palestinian and Jordanian assemblages; there are very few shared traits between north and south, the boundary being around the Dead Sea ('Amr and Schick 2001; Walmsley and Grey 2001). Exacerbating the situation is the apparent end of a monetary economy in the southern areas during the early sixth century, thereby removing from the archaeological record the useful chronological indicator of coins. Not surprisingly, then, pottery attributions in south Jordan can easily span two centuries, making secure site chronologies next to impossible.

Numismatics, government and social change

Numismatic research is acknowledged as a specialist field requiring an appreciation of style, considerable and often varied language skills, and a thorough historical perspective, and hence is commonly dealt with outside the main parameters of archaeology. On most archaeological projects the coins discovered during excavation are handed over to a numismatist, who provides identifications (dates, weights and mints especially) for the archaeologist, whose primary interest in the coins is usually as a dating tool for establishing absolute chronologies. However, coins can offer considerably more information on political structures and the economy, as has already been seen earlier in Chapter 2. There are, in addition, several complications in using coins for dating archaeological levels, and the naive application of chronological information based on coin identifications is an unfortunate characteristic of Near Eastern archaeology.

Early Islamic Syria-Palestine had a rich if complicated numismatic history spanning either side of historic reforms instigated by the caliph Abd al-Malik in the 690s, but only in recent years has a clearer picture of that problematical history been put together. Understanding much of the numismatic record of the seventh century was particularly challenging until the publication by Stephen Album and Tony Goodwin (2002) of a corpus of coins held in the Ashmolean Museum, the appreciation of which has been enhanced by Clive Foss (2004) and a further study by Goodwin (2005) based on the pre-reform coins held in the Khalili Collection. The chronology offered in these works convincingly supplants that previously proposed by Michael Bates (1976; 1986). Coinage of Syria-Palestine in the seventh century consisted of four major types: imported Byzantine, pseudo-Byzantine, Umayyad Imperial issues and the Standing Caliph series. The last three types were minted locally, and are known collectively as 'Arab-Byzantine' or, preferably, 'Pre-reform Islamic'. Most of the production was small copper change for the market place, but a few gold coins were issued under Abd al-Malik and, perhaps, earlier under Mu'awiyah. The last copper Byzantine issues to enter Syria-Palestine in any number were those minted under Constans II (r. 641-68) before 660, seemingly arriving as official shipments or through trade, perhaps both. Supply probably dried up with the foundation of the Umayyad caliphate. To meet everyday market needs, the first Islamic coppers were probably produced around this time, that is in the 650s to 660s or 670s. In size and imagery these coins were dependent on the issues of Constans II and hence gained the name 'pseudo-Byzantine', but there is no reason to doubt their legality as coinage.

A significant change in approach can be seen with the appearance of the following 'Umayyad Imperial Image' coin types (about 660-80, and hence overlapping with the 'pseudo-Byzantine' group), which in their size, weight and imagery display increasing central co-ordination at the provincial level. With these coins the image of the Byzantine emperor was deliberately replaced by a generalised imperial image, neither Byzantine emperor nor caliph. That substitution was to follow with the remarkable 'Standing Caliph' series (690s) of Abd al-Malik, with which the intention of producing a standardised and centralised coinage becomes abundantly clear. Similarities between provinces in iconography and metrology were much greater than differences, even if one province – The Jund al-Urdunn – opted out of this unified approach. Most variations were to do with presentation, and these largely conformed to the prevailing provincial structure. Within this series the first formal gold coinage was issued in Damascus between 693/4-696/7, also displaying an image of the standing caliph encircled by the *shahadah* (the proclamation of Faith: 'There is no god but God [Allah] alone; Muhammad is the messenger of God'). With this coin the caliph, the Prophet, God and His Message were all linked in one small, but significant, iconographic statement. Numismatic developments in Byzantium probably account for the introduction of an Islamic precious coinage, for until Abd al-Malik's reforms gold currency continued to be sourced from Byzantium. Hence the late seventh-century Nikertai hoard of gold coins found near Apamea consists of a spread of Byzantine issues dating from Maurice (582-602) to Constantine IV (668-85) (Morrisson 1972), as does the large Bet She'an (Baysan) hoard made up of issues from Phocas (602-10) to Constantine IV (Bijovsky 2002). The remarkable similarity in the coin supply pattern preserved in these two hoards and in a third from south Jordan demonstrates conclusively the formal nature of the sourcing and distribution of precious coin in seventh-century Syria-Palestine. The question then arises, what led to the abandoning of this convenient arrangement in about 690? The determined introduction of a gold denomination by Abd al-Malik in 693/4 was probably in response to the introduction of a representation of Christ holding the Gospels on the Byzantine solidus under Justinian II (685-95, 705-11), thereby associating the emperor with Christ, God and His Chosen Word. Abd al-Malik responded to this overtly Christian proclamation by creating an iconographical parallel with an alternative Muslim message of God/Allah, the Prophet Muhammad and the caliph.

The 'Standing Caliph' type was a necessary preliminary to the sweeping coinage reforms instigated by Abd al-Malik at the end of the seventh century. While the 'Standing Caliph' imagery emphasised the authority of the reigning caliph (in this case Abd al-Malik) by association with the Prophet Muhammad, a purely epigraphic reformed Islamic coinage sought authority primarily in the Qur'an and only by association with Prophet. It was, perhaps, a fatal move for the Umayyads as this ended the exclusive claim of their family to the caliphate and gave legitimacy to all other Muslims, even non-Arabs eventually, to aspire to the office of 'Commander of the Faithful' (*Amir al-Mu'minin*).

The post-reform coinage was issued in three major denominations: gold (*dinar*), silver (*dirham*) and copper (*fals*). All three were characterised by inscriptions in Kufic Arabic. Gold and silver coins included the *shahadah* to which were added extracts from the Qur'an referring to Allah and his Prophet Muhammad, arranged in central panels with encircling text. The marginal legend on the obverse included the year of minting according to the Muslim calendar and, with the dirhams, the place of manufacture. As the Umayyad administrative capital, Damascus was undoubtedly an important mint for both gold and silver in the first half of the eighth century. The introduction of a new tripartite monetary system was to have immediate implications for the monetary economy of Syria-Palestine. In a surprisingly short period of time the earlier gold coinage, Byzantine or pre-reform Islamic, was withdrawn from circulation in favour of the new post-reform denomination. Accordingly, hoards concealed in eighth-century Syria-Palestine consist overwhelmingly of dinars. Another major innovation emanating from Abd al-Malik's reforms was the large-scale minting and wide circulation of dirhams in Syria-Palestine, as silver coinage was rare in Byzantine times. With the coinage reforms, silver became fully integrated into the monetary economy of the region, becoming, in time, more significant than copper in the market place. As a result of its continuing regional application and declining value, copper coinage was considerably less uniform than gold or silver. In some instances the coins included vegetal and figural images, the latter not human but animals such as elephants, birds or lions, the significance of which is not clear.

Once the complexity of early Islamic coinage in Syria-Palestine is understood, the information it provides beyond setting chronological time-pegs for archaeologists is exceedingly valuable. From the first, hesitant, attempts at supplying the local economy with small change in the likeness of existing Byzantine currency, the rapid maturation of a specifically early Islamic coinage at the end of the seventh century reveals much broader social processes driven by the growing political consciousness of the Umayyad rulers. A dependence on Byzantine coinage and its imitations was replaced by a series of new coin issues increasingly independent of Byzantine concepts, although not completely divorced from them, only to be ultimately replaced by an immediately recognisable Islamic coinage overtly epigraphic in character. The process was, increasingly, from regional and informal to centralised and sanctioned, changes which were indicative of a progressively more institutionalised approach to governmental structures. Especially illuminating are the new gold coinages of the 690s. Of and for the elites and their client urban populations, these coins were formulated with a clear and intentional difference in the public message projected by each: the primacy of the message of the Qur'an and the Prophet Muhammad in Islam offset by the Byzantine Pantocrator bust of Christ, ruler of the universe. They are a testament to the first stage of a divergence in Muslim-Byzantine political relations inspired by the aspirations of two ruling classes and subsequently furthered by them, regardless of dynastic affiliation, on both sides. Nonetheless, in the face of an increasing standardisation of coin production local preferences were not ignored, as the later pre-reform and post-reform copper issues demonstrate through their continued adherence to regional standards in metrology and design. There is no question as to the brilliance and efficacy of Abd al-Malik's reforms; the new monetary system was to outlast him by centuries, in that the coin denominations thereby created were to circulate and be accurately replicated throughout much of the known world – from west and northern Europe to China – during the Islamic middle ages.

Coins can offer the archaeologist much more information that that already gleaned above. Accordingly, a number of other cases where coins can be used as a source of information on social and economic conditions in early Islamic Syria-Palestine will be described in the chapters that follow.

Craft goods, exotica and prestige items

A wide range of other objects in a variety of materials, for instance glass, metals, stone, bone and ivory, made up an extensive cultural inventory carried forward from late antiquity and, like the pottery and coinage, was increasingly adapted and reinvented into a recognisably Islamic cultural horizon in the later eighth to ninth centuries. Just as in earlier times in the Middle East, the conspicuous consumption of high-value luxury goods, often of exotic origin, became a hallmark of the upper echelon of Syro-Palestinian society, noticeably in the eighth century. As with the coins, these materials reveal the expanding presence of an emerging and confident ruling group within the context of an overall construction of an identifiably Islamic society in Syria-Palestine.

Recent work on glass has developed in two directions: defining an increasingly accurate typology of glass vessel shapes and their decoration from late antiquity into Fatimid times, and the investigation of technological innovations in Islamic-period glass production in north Syria. An understanding of the chronology of glass after the Islamic expansion was, until recent work, very rudimentary, and mostly restricted to glass weights and museum objects usually lacking any verifiable archaeological context. Latest studies into the glass from a series of excavations have identified significant variations in the corpus that now allow the separation of seventh-century glassware from that of the later eighth and beyond (O'Hea 2001; Pollak 1999). Seventh- and early eighth-century glass was commonly decorated with glass trails in contrasting colours, whereas vessels of the later eighth to ninth century were decorated with nipped patterns and applied like-coloured trails, after which followed material into the tenth century with liberally-applied pincer decoration. Distribution patterns of high-quality glassware also reveal interesting patterns, such as the confinement of high-relief cut vessels to seaport sites and the affinity of rare lustre-decorated and enamelled wares of Abbasid date with known Iraqi parallels, not Egyptian. The appearance of these fine glasswares in Syria-Palestine would seem to reflect a move to the market tastes of Iraq in the ninth century rather than the eighth, a cultural reorientation also seen in the ceramics (above).

In technological terms, the later eighth to ninth century also marked a revolutionary change in glass production (Henderson et al. 2004). The chemical analysis of glass pieces retrieved from a massive industrial complex of workshops and furnaces on the outskirts of Raqqah in north Syria identified the gradual abandonment of a pre-Islamic natron glass process and the adoption of plant ash as a substitute flux, a change only possible through the experimental courage and technological skill of the local artisans. Hence in the otherwise conservative craft of glass-making the early Islamic period was characterised by significant change in style and technology.

Metalwork similarly adapted to new market preferences in early Islamic Syria-Palestine, but as it is by its nature an easily re-usable commodity, surviving copper alloy products from early Islamic Syria-Palestine are quite rare. In the seventh and first half of the eighth centuries, Egypt appears to have been the major source of prestige metal objects for south Syria-Palestine. At Pella, a large brazier with drop handles and a fenestrated base was recovered from mid-eighth-century levels (Fig. 6), the direct parallels for which are found in Coptic Egypt. The spectacular Fudayn brazier, made by the lost-wax technique, featured four feet in the style of a griffin, corner figurines of naked females, and spirited decoration on the side panels in relief consisting of a six-arched columned arcade with a sequence of erotic scenes beneath each arch (Bisheh and Humbert 1997). Comparisons for this imagery are found in contemporary Coptic art, especially textiles and book illuminations, and it

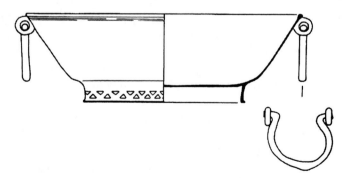

Fig. 6. Cosy heating: a fenestrated Egyptian-style brazier found in a mid-eighth-century house at Pella. Restored rim diameter: 38.5 centimetres; restored height: 12.8 centimetres (Pella Excavations/University of Sydney).

would seem that the rakish human and animal depictions in no way offended the sensibilities of the Muslim landlord of the early Islamic castle at Fudayn, located some 50 kilometres northeast of Amman. Other copper alloy objects from Fudayn included two hinged animal moulds, a censer and a spouted pot, while excavations at another Umayyad castle at Umm al-Walid south of Amman produced elaborately decorated censers and a three-footed juglet with an animal-headed spout (for Fudayn and Umm al-Walid see Museum with No Frontiers 2000: 51-2, 67-70, 91-2, 133-5). At the other end of the time scale, two extraordinary metal hoards of probable late tenth- or early eleventh-century date excavated at coastal Caesarea and inland Tiberias reveal the sophistication of household goods in the Fatimid period (Hirschfeld et al. 2000; Lester 1999). Lamp stands, candlesticks, buckets, ladles, ewers, bowls, trays, lidded boxes and braziers predominated, these being made by metal casting and sheet hammering and often decorated with anonymous benedictory inscriptions, floral scrolls, geometric patterns and animal figures. Stylistically, the metalwork belongs to an Egyptian-Syrian tradition, and reflects the functional requirements of households of the time: lighting, food preparation, eating, washing, heating and room deodorising, the latter an expensive but socially desirable exercise (for the use of these objects in houses, see Goitein 1983: 132-50).

The use of carved ivory and bone pieces as contrasting decorative inlays for dark wood furniture was the continuation of a long tradition in the region. Little of this craft has survived because of the fragile nature of the materials used, but one impressive example is a group of ivory panels recovered from the burnt reception room of the early Islamic palace at Humaymah in south Jordan (Foote and Oleson 1996). Probably the surviving parts of an elaborate chair (perhaps a throne), as some of the panels are curved as if meant to decorate an armrest, the finely executed low reliefs feature helmeted and

armoured soldiers in an unambiguous Persian style. They preserve a fascinating physical connection between Humaymah as
an estate of the Abbasid family and Persia's support of their
ultimately successful claim to the caliphate.

The incorporation of the Hijaz into a single Islamic polity in
the seventh century facilitated the dissemination of steatite
vessels into Syria-Palestine, and these items become common
in the repertoire of excavated material culture, especially in the
eighth to tenth centuries. Steatite was especially favoured for
the manufacture of objects where a level of heat tolerance and
retention was required, notably lighting, deodorising and cooking. From quarries in the northern Hijaz (Kisnawi et al. 1983:
78-9), steatite bowls, censers, lamps and, commonly, cooking
pots were transported to Syria-Palestine, with significant finds
at Aqabah and at sites along roads to the north, for instance
Amman, Fudayn, Jarash, Pella and Tabariyah. Further north,
steatite lamps and bowls were found in lesser numbers at Qasr
al-Hayr al-Sharqi and Hamah (Grabar et al. 1978: 187-8), but
perhaps not of material from the Hijaz based on available
descriptions of the stone characteristics. In the far north steatite objects are less common; there are some at Aleppo
(Gonnella 2006: 169), but at Rusafah 'green slate' is identified
rather than steatite (e.g. Mackensen 1984: 69, 70), probably
locally sourced. At many of the southern sites a chronological
sequence can be observed in the incised decoration on the
steatite vessels. Later eighth- and ninth-century forms are
notable for their elaborate incised decoration of rosettes, ar-
cades with lamps, circles, floral patterns and generalised
abstract designs, especially on vessels intended as inexpensive
substitutes for metal ones. What could be an explanation for
this burst of creative activity? As with the technological and
typological development of ceramics about the same time, the
growth of a decorative steatite industry can be seen as resulting
from the emergence of an expanded educated and merchant

group in early Islamic society. Households sought to acquire goods that emulated in function and, to some extent, appearance the high-value consumer goods in precious metals popular among the wealthier levels of society, a demand that was to be met by the creation of new industries and the expansion of trade (see Chapter 5).

Material culture, archaeology and early Islamic transformations

The cultural record of human society offers the archaeologist considerably more information than a mere chronology of the past. While accurate dating is critically important for establishing a reliable timeframe to map the progress of a society, the objective must be to look beyond mere chronology and the mapping of a sequence of facts – a higher goal unfortunately rare in all Middle Eastern archaeologies, not just that dealing with the Islamic periods. Interpreting the developments observable in the surviving material culture can help to identify and explain various cultural and economic paths taken by a society, in which continuity, discontinuity and change all play a part. In this chapter, the material record of early Islamic Syria-Palestine has been described and interpretations offered as to the meaning of the developments observed. In a range of object categories – pottery, coinage, glass, metalwork and stone – a shared pattern is discernible: modest development from pre-Islamic styles during the seventh century, a period of accelerated change from the end of the seventh century (coinage especially) extending into the first half of the eighth (ceramics), continuing development until the mid-eighth century and then a period of rapid and systemic change, involving elements of cultural discontinuity, in the later eighth and throughout the ninth century. This last phase was the most dramatic. Ceramics, glass, stone and perhaps metal working traditions with unbroken typological and technological lines stretching back centuries into antiquity were subjected to rigorous review; some were kept, others significantly modified or abandoned, while completely new methods and styles were introduced from distant lands. Here, from the perspective of material culture, was the dawn of the Islamic middle ages in Syria-Palestine.

4

Sites and settlement processes

Sites and settlement histories loom large in the archaeology of early Islamic Syria-Palestine. In some ways, the emphasis on sites is a legacy of 'classical' archaeology, which has traditionally focused on urban centres because of an obsession with culture, the arts and the supposed democratic institutions of towns, as manifested in both material (architectural) and cognitive (literary) sources. Secondly, the importance of site-studies is an historical legacy of the intellectual basis of research into late antiquity and early Islamic times; that is, a preoccupation with describing and explaining the perceived process of urban decay and site abandonment. Finally, studies of the Islamic heritage have focused on recording and categorising urban architecture, as outlined in Chapter 1. Although a proportionally excessive concern with site histories stemmed from such narrowly defined research objectives, which were further limited by the straightjacket of convention, there is little doubt that this work has demonstrated that towns continued to play a significant role in socio-economic life during early Islamic times. Hence there is a continuing need to analyse in some detail conditions in urban centres, but from a broader perspective that takes in the different social, cultural and economic roles they played after the rise of Islam.

This chapter deals with three decades of recent archaeological research and the advances offered by it in understanding site development and settlement profiles in Syria-Palestine after the rise of Islam. It should be noted, however, that many of the issues are anything but straightforward, and that clear answers are still elusive – and given current levels of knowledge are probably unattainable. The first part of this chapter evaluates the formal administrative hierarchy of Syria-Palestine in early Islamic times as briefly recorded in written sources, and the implications these sources hold for urban histories. The next part of the chapter looks at key sites where recent excavation and survey work has detailed urban developments after the Islamic expansion, in which the town is shown to be a dynamic, growing organism serving clearly defined local and interregional functions. Both established centres and new foundations are considered. The last part of the chapter deals with settlement processes in the countryside based on recent excavations and surveys. The importance of rural and landscape studies is strongly emphasised in contemporary archaeology, yet advances in this area remain especially deficient in Middle Eastern archaeology. Although a considerable majority of the population – probably something over 80 per cent – lived in the countryside, the ongoing focus on a purely urban history has ignored this large segment of the population, thereby limiting a fuller understanding of the period. In this chapter some consideration is given to this clearly important sector of the population, mostly though a consideration of rural settlement patterns in early Islamic times.

A formal urban hierarchy

The towns of Syria-Palestine served as the main focal points of cultural, religious and economic life for urban and rural populations alike in late antiquity, and this role continued unabated and without significant disruption after the Islamic expansion into the region. Towns, headed mostly by their bishops, negotiated a peaceful surrender that guaranteed civic and personal rights, leaving the Church in charge of day-to-day administration. As in Byzantine times, Syria-Palestine under a Muslim administration was split up into self-regulating provinces, each consisting of a principal and several secondary centres, but overall the number of provinces and districts was much reduced from earlier times and boundaries were redrawn. As a result, Syria-Palestine was subdivided into fewer provinces. The origins of a new administrative structure after the Islamic expansion are disputed. It could have been Sasanid (Whitcomb 1999), Heraclius-Byzantine (Shahîd 1987, 1989) or Byzanto-Arab (Haldon 1995) or very early Islamic (Walmsley 1987: 152-6), and perhaps a bit of each, but in its initial early Islamic form probably developed as a Muslim mirror of an emergency military system instituted by the Byzantine authorities during the 630s and subsequently modified under the first caliphs. While the formational process appears to be complex, the operation of the administrative apparatus in the first Islamic decades remained essentially the same, especially as most of the bureaucrats had also been in the employ of the Byzantines. Hence the language of administration was, at first, both Greek and Arabic, as confirmed by the informative bilingual tax demands for wheat and olive oil recovered at Nessana in the Negev (Kraemer 1958: 175-97). These tax documents show that a centralised and hierarchical system of government existed to a certain extent in Syria-Palestine before the reforms of Abd al-Malik (about 691), although the scale of this central authority continues to be disputed (Hoyland 2006). Requisitions of money, goods or services drawn up from central registers were addressed through church officials to the whole community, which had a collective responsibility to see that they were paid.

Other written information on the structure of the administration in early Islamic Syria-Palestine is not extant until the appearance of descriptive geographical works in Arabic dated to the ninth century (Dunlop 1971: 163-5). Meant as administrative manuals, not works of social science, these sources do preserve a reliable report on the provinces and main towns in each region of the Islamic world. However, as technical manuals these works are often little more than just name lists. The most complete source for Syria-Palestine in the early Abbasid period can be found in an official manual for government officials called *Kitab al-Masalik wa'l-Mamalik* (Book of Routes and Kingdoms) written by Ibn Khurdadhbih (826-913), in which the regions, administrative divisions, tax revenues and road system of the Islamic realm were outlined. In this book, Syria-Palestine is described as divided into five military provinces (*jund*, pl. *ajnad*), beginning with Palestine, Jordan and Damascus in the south and Hims and Qinnasrin in the north (Fig. 7). The border zone with Byzantium (*al-Awasim*) had a special status, especially under the Abbasids who campaigned annually into Anatolia. The capital for each province was situated away from the coast to protect it from Byzantine assault, with most being existing towns except that in Palestine, where a new foundation named al-Ramlah was established by the caliph Sulayman in about 715. Although there was much continuity, the redrawing of the provincial boundaries was accompanied by a change in status for some towns. Most noticeably the former provincial capitals of Antioch, Apamea and Scythopolis/Baysan lost their privileged status, being replaced by Chalcis/Qinnasrin, Emesa/Hims and Tabariyah/Tiberias respectively, although this change may have predated Islam depending on when the *ajnad* were formed. Such an alteration to a town's status clearly had a significant impact on its subsequent history, sometimes favourable, sometimes harmful depending on the nature of that change (Petersen 2005a; Walmsley 1987; Wheatley 2001: 123-6).

Containing considerably more detail on the towns of Syria-Palestine is a much-acclaimed tenth-century geography by al-Maqdisi (d. 1000), the *Kitab Ahsan at-Taqasim fi Ma'rifat*

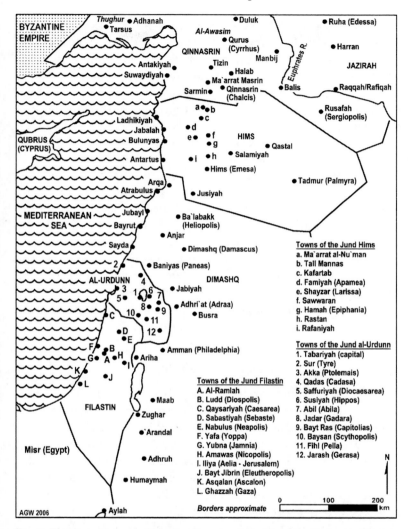

Fig. 7. The five-province administrative structure (the *ajnad*) of early Islamic Syria-Palestine, after *c.* 685, based on ninth-century Arabic geographical sources (Walmsley).

75

al-Aqalim (*Book of the Best Divisions for Knowledge of the Regions*), which was completed by 985. As a work of geography it was undoubtedly exceptional for its age, offering a 'modern' overview of the Islamic world (Dunlop 1971: 165-7; Wheatley 2001: 62-7). As a native of Jerusalem, al-Maqdisi's description of Syria-Palestine was especially thorough, although neither exhaustive nor complete. He subdivided the region into six districts (*kurah*) called, from north to south, Qinnasrin, Hims, Damascus, Jordan, Palestine and al-Sharah. Damascus was the regional capital, with district capitals at Aleppo, Hims, Tabariyah, al-Ramlah and Sughar (Zughar). Each district had other major centres serving widely differing roles, from administrative to commercial and military (Wheatley 2001: 112-26). Maqdisi's reasons for including, or excluding, places in this last group varied, and not all had been important in earlier centuries. In some instances his knowledge of certain geographical areas seemed inadequate, such as north Jordan, probably due to travel limitations imposed by the disturbed political situation in Syria-Palestine during the tenth century.

Urban archaeology

An abundance of new archaeological discoveries in the last few decades has greatly transformed perceptions of conditions in towns of all categories, from highly placed provincial capitals to minor district centres. In all cases a much more dynamic urban environment can be identified and characterised at both the intra-site and inter-site level. Nevertheless, the continuous occupation of many important sites down to the present has created a major problem for Islamic archaeology in Syria-Palestine. In most modern cities, for instance Damascus, Aleppo and Amman, the places available for exploration are severely curtailed, sometimes impossibly so. Whereas a great deal is known about the citadel area of Amman, for example, precious little material is available on parallel developments in downtown Amman. Hence the potentially 'best' cases for the construction of regional urban histories are often missing from the equation. Nevertheless, the situation is improving, as is explained below.

Existing towns: tradition, additions and renewal

Unlike Iraq, Syria-Palestine was not subjected to mass immigration by Arab tribes after the Islamic expansion, probably in part due to the high number of Arabs already living in the region (Donner 1981: 245-50). Those who did move to Syria-Palestine during or immediately after the Islamic expansion found sufficient space in existing towns. Such space resulted from a variety of factors: flight of inhabitants, limited but more common in north Syria closer to the Byzantine border; the availability of derelict urban areas waiting for refurbishment, perhaps more than usual due to recent calamities such as earthquake and plague; and confiscation of houses by treaty on occasions. In some places, new settlers could also move into existing settlements (*hadir*) established next to major towns by Arab tribes in pre-Islamic times, for instance at Qinnasrin. The end result was very positive for the major towns of Syria-Palestine and, in some instances, secondary centres also, and these benefits can often be observed in the archaeological record. Two parallel, rather than contradictory, trends can be observed in the urban history of established towns after the Islamic expansion: the maintenance of existing civic traditions inherited from late antiquity and, at the same time, the introduction of new ideas about the essential components of a town. It was a the bringing together of an old urban tradition with new but already formulated expectations that, once combined, was to work very well.

One town that experienced considerable growth after the

Islamic expansion was Tabariyah, the capital of the al-Urdunn (Jordan) province located on the western shore of Lake Tiberias (see Fig. 7). A marked expansion of settlement activity beginning in the eighth century has been observed in the archaeological record at different locations in and around Tiberias, even if the exploration of the site has been somewhat erratic and unsystematic as a result of modern expansion. Excavations in the mid-1970s, only recently published, around the southern city gate exposed shops and houses first erected in the eighth century and in use until the eleventh, while two-storeyed, central-courtyard domestic units expanded over a former cemetery and open land on the road southwards to Hammam Tabariyah, thereby joining the two sites into one large metropolis (Stacey 2004).

Elsewhere evidence for workshops and other commercial activities were uncovered. At Hammam Tabariyah, the site of a bathhouse built over a natural hot spring, an apsidal synagogue with a sequence of impressive polychrome mosaic floors was excavated in the 1960s, with evidence for ongoing use as a place of worship in the first Islamic centuries (Dothan and Johnson 2000). In the last period of use (Stratum 1a, Abbasid and probably later) the prayer hall received its final mosaic while the space around the synagogue was subdivided into shops, residential units and a classroom. Another synagogue, rebuilt after a major earthquake in 749 and with occupation until the eleventh century, was uncovered in the northern part of the town. Excavations between 1989 and 1994 have exposed further evidence of burgeoning urban activity at Tiberias between the eighth and eleventh centuries, with repeated evidence for urban renewal after the mid-eighth-century earthquake (Hirschfeld 2004b: 3-71). In the western lower town, stone-built dwellings of the eighth century were uncovered, built over the ruins of an earlier structure of uncertain purpose that was destroyed in the 749 earthquake. The replacement buildings were clearly domestic;

plain yet functional. The main unit, measuring about 8.35 by 9.0 metres, was originally planned as two small houses that were subsequently combined into a single dwelling. One of the original houses featured a plain but attractive coloured mosaic floor, with a central medallion featuring intertwining bands. Glazed pottery, decorated ceramic lamps, glass including moulded and incised types, an array of copper alloy objects, and bone pins and buttons provide an informative insight into the better than modest repertoire that made up the cultural assemblage in the poorer houses of Islamic Tabariyah.

Excavations undertaken at a Justinianic church on the summit of Mount Berenice, overlooking the lower town, have revealed parallel results. The original church was destroyed in the 749 earthquake, only to be rebuilt and continuously used – although with modifications – into the Crusader period (Hirschfeld 2004b: 75-227). Recent discoveries in the lower town, notably the stockpile of copper alloy vessels mentioned in the last chapter, have further illustrated the ongoing privileged status of Tabariyah well beyond the ninth century. Collectively, the archaeology of Islamic Tabariyah reveals the considerable economic gains that flowed from the town's promotion to the provincial capital of the Jund al-Urdunn. Significantly, these benefits continued with little interruption despite two potential set backs in the mid-eighth century: a devastating earthquake in 749 CE and, in the following year, the forceful overthrow of the Umayyad caliphate in Syria-Palestine.

Further north, the site of Hadir Qinnasrin, in due course the capital of the Jund Qinnasrin, offers a most interesting example of the transformation from pre-Islamic tribal encampment (*hirah*) to a permanent settlement of late antiquity (*hadir*), and thence to an Islamic town (*misr*) designed to fulfil the social, cultural and religious requirements of the *jund's* Muslim population (Whitcomb 2000a). Situated next to the large Hellenistic and Roman town of Chalcis, which served as a major military centre in late antiquity, the Hadir Qinnasrin was an Arab encampment of the Tanukh and Tayyiʿ tribes that, with the arrival of Islam, functioned as the obvious focal point for the new administration. Under Muʿawiyah, additional settlers were introduced from the Iraqi towns of Kufah and Basra, after which his successor Yazid (680-3) converted the *hadir* into a *misr* by erecting walls and locating the administration for a new province, the Jund Qinnasrin, in the town. According to Donald Whitcomb (2000a: 26-8), this process of conversion from transient to permanent settlement is recognisable in the archaeological record. His excavations uncovered an independent, two-roomed dwelling that reflected in layout the traditional arrangement of the long, goat-hair tents of Arab nomads, in plan an elongated rectangle split internally into two sections, each serving different social functions and gender roles. While the evidence is still tantalisingly incomplete, Whitcomb's thesis does emphasise the importance of planning in the first Islamic settlements of Syria-Palestine, as military encampments became transformed, through brick, stone and wood, into permanent foundations. The implication is that behind the Qinnasrin sequence stood a long tradition of symmetry in the settlement history of pre-Islamic Arabia, an order based on an understanding of the functional and aesthetic benefits resulting from the adoption of a planned layout for each new foundation, *hadir* to *misr* or, as we shall see below, *misr* alone.

Particularly detailed insights into urban developments during early Islamic times has come from comprehensive archaeological work at Jerusalem and Rusafah, neither of which were major administrative capitals but both of which were highly significant in Umayyad socio-political policy in the eighth century. In addition to the major monumental embellishments of the exquisite Dome of the Rock and the Aqsa Mosque on the Haram al-Sharif (the 'Noble Enclosure', the rebuilt Temple Mount of the Jews, about which the literature

is extensive; see recently, Ettinghausen et al. 2001: 15-20),
Jerusalem was provided with a major complex of five stone-
built two-storeyed courtyard buildings immediately south and
west of the Haram al-Sharif (Ben-Dov 1985: 293-321). The
largest building, which measured 96 by 84 metres, was entered
by way of gates on the north, east and west, from which passage
ways led to the central porticoed courtyard. Flanking the court
on all sides were deep halls, those on the north interconnected,
an arrangement reminiscent of an inn or storage magazine
rather than a palace, the suggested function of this building by
the excavator. The discovery of many decorated marble architectural elements and plastered blocks with painted abstract
designs indicate possible living quarters on the upper floor, but
the Spartan standards adopted for the decoration further indicate a pilgrims' hostel rather than accommodation for nobility.
Another of the buildings was a large bathhouse, also designed
to serve a large number of people.

Another place that benefited greatly from Umayyad patronage was Rusafah in north Syria, home of the popular
martyr-saint Sergius and much favoured by the emperor Justinian and the Arab Christian Ghassanid allies of the
Byzantines alike (Shahîd 1995: 949-62; 2002: 115-33). Here the
caliph Hisham (r. 724-43) relocated his royal residence for part
of the year at least (and here was buried), thereby instigating a
huge building programme (Haase 1995). A large, courtyard-
style congregational mosque was constructed abutting the
famous Basilica of the Holy Cross, adjacent to which was constructed a small market (*suq*) that linked mosque and church
(Sack 1996; Ulbert 1986; 1997). Deliberate planning and order
within an existing urban framework is immediately apparent
in the plan (Fig. 8), ensuring the continued importance of the
mosque-church-market grouping well after the overthrow of
the Umayyads in 750. Work in the last few years by Dorothée
Sack and colleagues has identified numerous courtyard build-

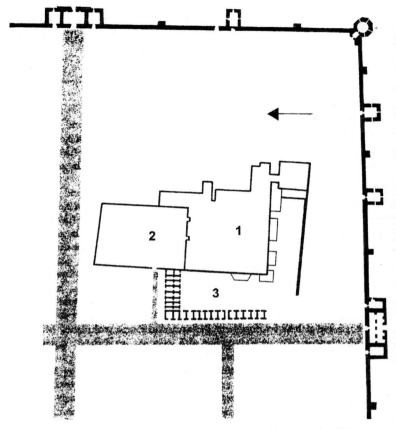

Fig. 8. Plan of the church (1), mosque (2) and *suq* complex (3)
at Rusafah, Syria (after Ulbert 1997).

ings, each of a good size, spread around without the walled
enclosure of Rusafah, which are to be associated with Hisham's
formal residence complex of decorated palaces and outbuildings
located south of the town (Sack and Becker 1999).

As the examples presented here demonstrate, it should come
as no surprise that the major centres of Syria-Palestine were
the recipients of concerted attention co-ordinated by an

Umayyad administration, and that many of these places served an ongoing role as social, administrative and commercial centres after the end of the dynasty. This situation has been recognised for some time, with recent work confirming and expanding understanding of these developments. Especially significant is the identification of a major Arab Islamic contribution to the urban history of Syria-Palestine that originated in pre-Islamic practices in the Arabian Peninsula. The towns were, accordingly, not the product of a solitary lineal process carried forward from late antique Syria-Palestine, and did not evolve unitarily out of one standardised form into another. Rather than evolutionary, the path was ancestral: an origin, augmented with many layers of additional urban traditions until the contributions came to outweigh the beginnings and transform the ancestral core. This was, more correctly, the nature of a developing early Islamic urbanism in Syria-Palestine.

While a strong case from archaeology can be made for the continuing relevance of the major towns of Syria-Palestine, less attention has been paid to secondary centres, the assumption being, until recently, that these places did poorly after the arrival of Islam. Hence Alastair Northedge was to write of three smaller towns in the Jund al-Urdunn:

> The evidence of the excavations at Jerash and Pella, or Baisan on the West Bank ... has shown considerable continued small-scale construction and many finds under the Umayyads, but little monumental construction and no large mosques. The picture reflects the accounts in the historical sources of heavy taxation, and probably demonstrates that these cities remained largely non-Muslim until their abandonment (Northedge 1999: 1083-5).

The problem has been that a shortage of dependable data and misleading conclusions deduced from earlier, erratic, archaeological work have combined to create a negative impression of urban conditions in the regional centres of early Islamic Syria-Palestine. Often it has been argued that places such as Baysan, Pella and Jarash were but ghosts of their former greatness, living on past glory. So not only Alastair Northedge, but also Hugh Kennedy (1999) and Wolfgang Liebeschuetz (2000: 47-50, 56), argue for a diminutive Jarash in Islamic times, little more than a putrid urban skeleton left behind after the decay of a once respectable 'Roman' metropolis. At issue, in fact, is the accuracy of current interpretations of urban life in early Islamic Syria-Palestine, and specifically the situation at Jarash. Was it no more than a town of only 'some prosperity' with a mosque 'little more than a large room with a mihrab in the shadow of the giant remains of antiquity and large numbers of Christian churches' (Kennedy 1999: 229)? In other words, was the urban expression of a new Islamic presence at Jarash solely to be found in little more than a few Roman-period stones miserly and ineffectively shuffled about?

Certainly not, for the 2002 discovery of a large, centrally-placed congregational mosque at Jarash has required the outright rejection of such impressionistic and obsolete perceptions, and necessitated a completely new approach to describing and explaining urban transformations during the first Islamic centuries in Syria-Palestine. Jarash's principal mosque was constructed in a prominent location, immediately southwest of the plaza and monument that marked the cross-road of the town's primary streets (Fig. 9). It replaced a bathhouse that before demolition had been converted into an industrial complex, similar to functional changes made at a bathhouse in central Baysan. The stone-built mosque would have been an imposing sight, but one that was in sympathy with the existing urban vista inherited from classical times. Measuring almost 40 metres east-west and nearly 45 metres north-south, the mosque conformed to the so-called 'courtyard'

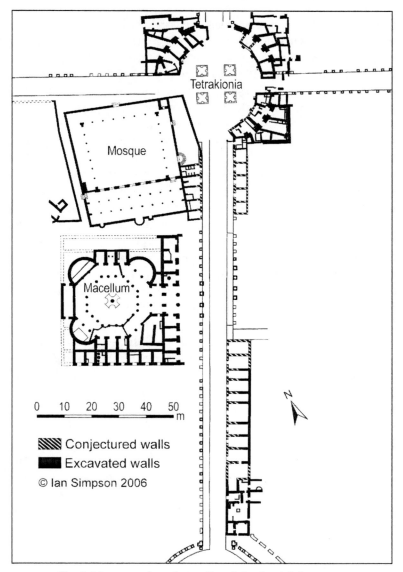

Fig. 9. Mosque and market at Jarash in the eighth century
(© I. Simpson 2006).

type with columned porticoes on three sides and a deeper,
hypostyle hall with a double colonnade on the fourth (southern)
side, where the congregation assembled for prayers. The southern wall featured an axial primary prayer niche, the *mihrab*,
and two later smaller recesses. The main doorway into the
mosque was located in the middle of the north wall, allowing
entry from an east-west street of continuing importance. However, this entrance soon proved impractical and a grand
semi-circular staircase was included midway on the east wall
to facilitate entry from Jarash's main north-south street, which
in early Islamic times served as the market place (*suq*) of
Jarash. A notable feature was the angle at which the mosque
was constructed in relation to the Roman-period urban grid, a
result of attempting to get the key south wall of the mosque to
face the Holy City of Makkah, a requirement of all mosques.
The offset orientation of the mosque could have created an
eyesore on the north and east sides where the mosque faced out
on existing streets, but the problem was ingeniously solved by
disguising the discrepancy. On the east side a line of new shops
was built between street and mosque, thereby masking an
uncomfortable divergence in the architecture as the façades of
the new shops were aligned to the Roman-period grid. Not only
did this solution show the desire of Jarash's inhabitants to
maintain urban symmetry, it also underlined the ongoing
importance of markets in the towns of early Islamic Syria-
Palestine. The careful expansion of the shops encircling the
south tetrakionia also displays a desire to preserve urban symmetry (Fig. 9). While, therefore, the Jarash mosque was
seamlessly accommodated into the urban layout of Jarash, it
also left unaffected the predominantly Christian character of
the town. Its many churches continued in use right through the
Umayyad period, only to be suddenly destroyed in the mid-
eighth century by a violent act of nature – an earthquake – as
graphically revealed during the excavation of the Church of St

Theodore by the Yale Joint Mission in the 1930s (Crowfoot 1938: 223-4). The severity of this seismic event was recently confirmed by the discovery of a human victim entombed in a collapsed building along with his mule, some possessions and a hoard of 143 silver dirhams of mostly eastern origin, the last of which was minted in the year of the earthquake.

In recent years, the other sites named by Northedge for their supposed lacklustre urban life (Baysan and Pella) have also revealed evidence for considerable urban activity, including significant construction (a reminder that it is never safe to argue from negative evidence in archaeology). For Pella, the evidence is most conclusive following the demolition of the town in the earthquake of 749. Governmental and economic imperatives required a replacement for the pulverised late antique/ early Islamic town centre located next to the main church, a need met by the construction of two large, double-storey compounds immediately northeast of the devastated town (Walmsley 1991). Each consisted of a sizeable central courtyard surrounded by rooms, some for living and others for storage, while one area was devoted to glass production. No doubt the total occupied area of the site was reduced (what percentage of these sites was ever fully utilised in any case?), but activity was still considerable.

At Baysan, a major restoration of the urban infrastructure in the Umayyad period included the construction of a new row of shops, but this upgrade of the urban environment was only belatedly identified as belonging to the caliphate of Hisham following the unexpected discovery of two dedicatory mosaic panels in Arabic (Khamis 2001; Tsafrir and Foerster 1997: 123, 138-40). Initially interpreted as Byzantine based on epigraphic evidence, a major component of the refurbishment was the construction of around 20 shops linearly arranged along a street and prefaced with a portico some 4.5 metres deep, but hardly an arrangement that can be termed an 'oriental bazaar'

(Tsafrir and Foerster 1997: 138). The shops replaced an earlier public structure, a basilical hall, destroyed by an earthquake, perhaps that of 659-60. That same earthquake, also known from graphic archaeological evidence at Pella just across the Jordan Valley from Baysan (Watson and Tidmarsh 1996), was probably responsible for the collapse of the large centralised church on the summit of Baysan's ancient tell. In its place a large double-compound encircled by a wall was built as the Umayyad governmental centre for Baysan (Fitzgerald 1931; Walmsley f.c. [2007b]). The complex featured an outer circuit wall pierced by a stout gate, and streets flanked by housing, finishing at an inner walled enclosure, probably the palace, entered by a gate flanked by waiting benches.

The Baysan administrative complex is paralleled conceptually and physically at Amman, although the structure at Amman was executed in a much grander scale befitting the role of the town as a sub-governorship of Damascus in early Islamic times. In the 1980s, Alastair Northedge undertook a detailed re-analysis of a monumental palatial complex on the citadel of Amman, celebrated because of a cruciform gateway lavishly decorated with niches featuring carved vegetal and geometric patterns. In his study, Northedge (1992) demonstrated unequivocally an early Islamic, probably Umayyad, date for its construction. Recent large-scale excavations by a Spanish mission has revealed that the palace is but one part of a much larger urban conglomerate with distinct functional zones, consisting of streets, a market plaza, a mosque, houses, a bathhouse and water systems servicing a self-contained, compact town imposingly set above the late antique and early Islamic centre below – what could be termed a *madinah 'supra' madinah* (Almagro and Arce 2001; Walmsley f.c. [2007b]). Abbasid-period restoration of the complex was recognised by Northedge (1992: 158-9, described as 'modest'), and the mosque as it survives is distinctly eastern ('Persian') in plan and decoration, and perhaps also represents a later refurbishment, if not complete reconstruction.

Two other sites have produced clear evidence for market construction in the first half of the eighth century, matching the significant discoveries at Baysan. At Palmyra, a water-rich oasis midway between Hims and the Euphrates and famous for its impressive Roman-period architecture, a 180-metre long line of shops was erected along the main colonnaded street consisting of 45 units divided into two sections (As'ad and Stepniowski 1989). The new line of shops opened northwards onto a lane, roughly the width of the earlier footpath of the street, and thereby faced the original shops, still in use, on the north side of the street. A large commercial complex was thus created, consisting of an axial walkway some seven metres wide and flanked on both sides by a near-continuous line of around 100 shops. The complex continued to be utilised into Abbasid times. On the Mediterranean coast at Arsuf, a linear shopping street was likewise built sometime in the eighth century, but this time as a completely new project (Roll and Ayalon 1987). The street had a long and productive history, probably not ending until the Crusades, with eight major superimposed street levels being detected.

In north Syria existing towns also received attention. Recent excavations within Aleppo's famous Ayyubid citadel (later twelfth to thirteenth century) has uncovered evidence of Umayyad-period settlement, confirming an account in written sources of the rebuilding of the citadel walls following an earthquake (Gonnella 2006: 168-9). Likewise the mound at Hamah apparently was walled (or re-walled) in the eighth century (Ploug 1985: 109-11), and although Ploug opts for a Byzantine date an Umayyad one fits better. It would seem that the construction of circuit walls on highpoints to create an early type of Islamic citadel above existing towns began in the Umayyad period, as evidenced at Amman, Baysan, Hamah and Aleppo. These strongholds, however, were more symbolic than military in intent.

Overall, the evidence is compelling: under the Umayyads, especially during the first half of the eighth century, established regional centres benefited from targeted programmes of urban renewal, including mosque building, administrative complexes and commercial infrastructure. Some of these projects were instigated high up in the administration (or at least attributed to senior administrators); others appear to have been local initiatives. In this, the structure of patronage was not much different from that of late antiquity.

Nevertheless, doubts remain as to the urban health of some centres, especially in the southern reaches of Syria-Palestine. In a recent study of Petra, Zbigniew Fiema (2002) continues to express grave doubt as to the site's viability after late antiquity, arguing that the early Islamic period was the age of Petra's 'decline'. However, parallels with an earlier urban history for the late antique towns of north Jordan (see above, Chapter 1) would suggest that the gap is, in part at least, a knowledge-based one, not one that accurately reflects settlement history in the region. The earlier confusion surrounding the destruction date of the Petra church is indicative of attitude-based deductions that continue to dominate archaeological research in south Jordan; hence only the discovery of dated papyri in the church complex led to any serious questioning of the 551 date initially proposed for that building's destruction. Furthermore archaeological work has shown that other sites in the region, such as Arandal/Arindela and Adhruh/Augustopolis, had unbroken histories into early Islamic times and well beyond (Schick 1994; Walmsley and Grey 2001).

New establishments

In pre-modern terms, Syria-Palestine in antiquity was heavily urbanised, creating a settlement profile of towns and surrounding territory suited to the rugged terrain of the region. As

already noted (Chapter 1), this profile extended into late antiquity and was barely touched at the regional level by the
Sasanid incursion or the Islamic expansion of the early seventh
century. Hence there was little demand for a new round of
urban growth after the arrival of Islam, yet the seventh and
especially eighth centuries did witness the creation of new
settlements, some of which were urban in both intent and size.
Many of the others were more localised developments, sometimes modelled on urban principles, directly resulting from the
activities of a royal patron (Bacharach 1996). To this group
belong the so-called 'desert castles', found spread throughout
much of Syria-Palestine, which have been the subject of much
scholarly debate. It is, nevertheless, important to view these
foundations as part of a wider policy of settlement development
in the early Islamic period, a policy in keeping with the seden-
tary practices of the Christian Ghassanids in the sixth century
and, in some cases, involving the refurbishment of Ghassanid
structures in the Syrian steppe such as Qasr al-Hayr al-Gharbi
and Hallabat (Shahîd 2002: 375-91).

The various attributes that characterised urban improvements in early Islamic Syria-Palestine were brought together
into one programme with the foundation of several new regional centres, each deliberately planned with specific
functions in mind and strategically placed in an already urban-
rich region. These centres were conceived as 'complete' urban
entities, some being established as independent centres while
others were intentionally sited next to existing towns. In them
can be seen a nascent Islamic urbanism, experimental and
confident yet springing from formulated ideas. Their existence
negates the oft-stated yet misleading assertion that the Muslims rarely founded new towns in Syria-Palestine, a claim
deceptively backed by categorising a number of foundations as
palatial estates rather than urban in intent. Fortunately, a
number of these new centres are reasonably well preserved and

have been subjected to detailed archaeological investigation in recent years, although with mixed results.

Clearly significant among the early Islamic foundations in Syria-Palestine was a new provincial capital for Filastin (Palestine) initiated by the Umayyad caliph Sulayman (r. 715-17). Named al-Ramlah, supposedly after the sandy nature of the area, this town was to succeed like no other place in Syria-Palestine founded during the early Islamic period, as a result of its strategic and economic importance as much as of its administrative role. However, Ramlah's long and complicated history until modern times has meant that the site's original features, including its most famous landmark, the 'White Mosque', have been greatly obscured by centuries of human activity, and recent work has made little progress in clarifying the plan of the early Islamic settlement. Useful but hypothetical is an attempt by Nimrod Luz (1997) to reconstruct the layout of the site (see also Whitcomb 1995b: 491-2), whereas earlier work in the field had identified individual elements of the town but had not contributed to an overall understanding (Gibson and Vitto 1999; Petersen 2005a: 95-102). Fortunately, major salvage excavations by the Israel Antiquities Authority in the last few years have begun to clarify the urban limits and individual features of the site, including the town's principal aqueduct. Recently, the discovery of houses and shops was announced on the Israel Antiquities Authority's website, in which numerous ceramic, glass and metal objects, including a juglet containing gold coins (*dinars*) of the eighth to eleventh centuries were found. Other metal objects included copper alloy weights, a balance from the shops and bracelets in gold and silver inscribed with benedictions. Together these finds reveal a high level of wealth and economic activity at early Islamic Ramlah, a situation not unexpected for the chief town of Filastin.

Better preserved is Anjar, located in the Biqa Valley of Lebanon, yet even after half a century of excavation and research this site remains an enigmatic and puzzling foundation of the early eighth century. At first sight Anjar presents as something of an anomaly, falling somewhere between town and rural estate, given the site's overall size and the variety of architecture it contains. Accordingly, Anjar has been analysed from the perspective of a new urban foundation straddling antiquity and the Islamic middle ages (Hillenbrand 1999), but also as a landed estate monumentalised by a palatial complex complete with a full complement of support buildings of mosque, bath, water systems, markets and residential units (Whitcomb 1994a: 19). In this, Anjar drew strongly on the existing urban traditions of late antiquity, but played with them inventively, mostly successfully. Within towered walls measuring 370 by 310 metres, cross-streets ran between four centrally placed gateways, thereby dividing the interior into four sizeable quadrants. The streets, lined with shops and colonnades (see the cover photograph), meet in the centre at an impressive monument composed of four bases each of which supported four lofty monolithic columns – a classicising *tetrakionia*. Each quadrant was further subdivided with great symmetry, and consisted of co-ordinated public zones of palace, mosque, administrative building, bathhouse, courtyards and private residential units neatly ordered around 'a truly Manhattanised street grid' (Hillenbrand 1999: 85). Neither late antique nor Islamic, Anjar hovered somewhere in between, but not evenly so; some attributes barely diverge from a classical tradition – the *tetrakionia* for instance – whereas others were quite new, notably the unobstructed disposition of the mosque-palace complex at the social heart of the town. Anjar's intended function remains difficult to explain, probably because it was created to perform a multiplicity of purposes: town, fort, a hub for trade and agricultural projects, an entrepôt for Damascus, occasional royal residence and, in social terms, an 'instrument of colonisation' (Hillenbrand 1999: 93). Essentially, Anjar contains all of the elements found with the extensive palatial complex of Amman – a virtual, purposive 'mini-city' – but relocated in a rich rural context. Functionally, the complex of buildings at Qasr al-Hayr al-Sharqi would have served a similar function, but at that site the palace stood independent of, yet juxtaposed to, the main walled enclosure with its mosque and formal units (Grabar et al. 1978). Combined, these parts made up a *madinah*, as a lost inscription from the site asserted, a new foundation on the Rusafah-Palmyra road at or close to the shared border of Hims and Qinnasrin. In all of these cases the intended message, socially and politically, must have been very similar to the palatial complexes in existing towns, although the pastoral and largely nomadic audience of the steppe was addressed anew in a way of specific relevance to the Umayyads.

An informative parallel to Ramlah and Anjar, even if somewhat smaller in size, is the walled site of Aylah at Aqabah in Jordan. Excavated between 1986 and 1992 by Donald Whitcomb (1988a: 14-15; 1995b), the new foundation was conceived as a *misr* ('encampment') next to an existing settlement (Roman-Byzantine Ailana), and inherited its companion site's name in the form of Aylah. Laid out as a 167 by 134 metre rectangle, Aylah was equipped with particularly imposing circuit walls featuring large corner towers and projecting U-shaped intervening towers, a style inspired by south Jordan and Egyptian Roman military encampments but, with Aylah, more for show than defence (Whitcomb 2006). In the centre of each wall was a broad arched gateway flanked by towers, that on the west being highlighted by a Qur'anic inscription to greet the annual pilgrimage caravan from Egypt. Inside the gate stood an entrance vestibule, exited by way of a second arch. Internally, the layout of the settlement was determined by two axial cross-streets between the gates with a *tetrapylon* (four-way gate) at the junction, although the resultant orthogonal

94

plan was greatly modified by a long history of occupation until the Crusades. In later times, but perhaps originally, the streets were relatively narrow and plain, lined with shops but lacking porticos. Rather, the overwhelmingly dominant architectural feature within the walls was a large congregational mosque noticeably wider than deep both before and after its relocation westwards in the later eighth or early ninth century, a move made possible by deflecting also to the west the street between the *tetrapylon* and the north gate. Questionable is Whitcomb's suggested foundation date of around 650 for the walled settlement, that is during the caliphate of Uthman b. Affan (644-56, Whitcomb 1989: 167-75; 2006: 65-7), for while the possibility of a provisional encampment at this spot is feasible (a settlement process from transitory to permanent entertained elsewhere by Whitcomb, 2000a: 10-12, 26-8), an Umayyad date, either later seventh or early eighth century, would seem much more likely for the foundation of a permanent *misr*.

Some architectural confirmation of a later date for Aylah can be found in the results of recent work at the castle-township site of al-Bakhra, near Palmyra in the Syrian Desert, infamous as the site of al-Walid II's assassination in 744. Originally founded as a Roman-period fort, it was enlarged by the addition of a new quarter in the 680s, this being encased within a wall with rounded towers (Fig. 10). Its resultant size 'places it in the category of the new urban settlement, rather than as a single *qasr*' (Genequand 2004a; 2006: 12), but, as will be discussed below, the line between the two – town or castle – remains very difficult to draw. Around the walled compound at al-Bakhra are the remains of numerous structures reminiscent of the development at Umayyad Rusafah, including large enclosures in clusters to the north, probably the site of a *fustat* (encampment) known from historical sources, and village houses and funerary monuments in a group to the south and east. A church and adjoining mosque, the latter perhaps of an early lateral type,

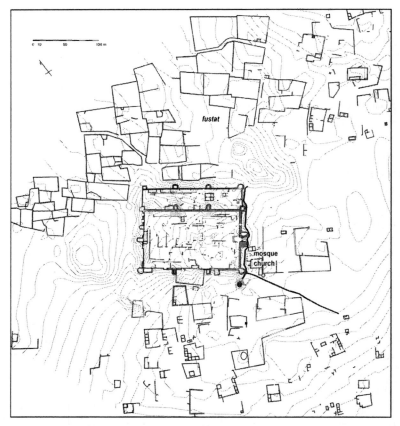

Fig. 10. Plan of al-Bakhra, Syria (after Genequand 2004a: 228).

stood to the southeast of the walled compound. In all, the combined site of fort, *extra-muros* village and *fustat* covered some 750 by 600 metres, or 40 hectares.

A number of completely new foundations with clear urban aspirations were set up in the Jazirah ('island') region of north Syria between the Euphrates and Tigris rivers. Created as the centre piece of a large agricultural project, their purpose was economic, political and, especially in the north, military. Until recently, the widespread use of mudbrick as a building material, unlike stone in the south, and its higher rate of decay have resulted in less attention being paid to these sites. At Madinat al-Far in the Balikh valley north of al-Raqqah, the prince, provincial governor and general Maslamah b. Abd al-Malik (d. 738-39) built a 330-metre square compound with gates and walls, to which was added in a later, probably Abbasid, time a larger, more randomly organised complex of mansions subsequently enclosed within a second wall (Haase 2006). This expansion was probably related to Abbasid policies towards Byzantium, especially the formation of the *thughur* and the undertaking of annual expeditions into Anatolia. The family of Maslamah did not fare as badly as many other Umayyads after the overthrow of the dynasty and this is reflected in continued occupation at the site until at least the later ninth century. Similar but larger at *c.* 650 by 650 metres is the eighth- to tenth-century site of Kharab Sayyar, located east of Madinat al-Far (Meyer 2006). Gates, two each in the north and south walls and one each in the east and west walls, gave access into the town through towered walls, inside which has been identified a large mosque and a *suq* (both recognised in 2002 through magnetometer survey), palaces, baths, water systems and large house complexes of stucco-decorated rooms around central courtyards. Added to these facilities was a caravanserai, located outside the walls to the northwest.

In north Syria the benefits of patronage outlasted the Umayyads. The site of Raqqah (classical Nikephorion), located on the junction of the Euphrates and Balikh rivers, first found favour under the caliph Hisham, who built an agricultural estate next to the city (perhaps to supply nearby Rusafah). Under the Abbasids, an entirely new city was constructed by the caliph al-Mansur (754-75) to the west of al-Raqqah and called al-Rafiqah, 'the companion', which in time assumed the name of its older neighbour. In plan the new city copied, to some extent, the then recently completed city of Madinat al-Salam (Baghdad), but at al-Raqqah/al-Rafiqah formed a parallelogram surmounted by a half circle 1.3 kilometres wide, all within a gated circuit wall some five kilometres long. Soon after, in 796, the caliph Harun al-Rashid (r. 786-809) made the twin cities his capital, staying there for twelve years.

Work by Syrian and German teams over many years at the site has uncovered major new evidence on the layout of al-Rafiqa. Located in the centre of the town was a Great Mosque of monumental proportions (108 by 93 metres), which was constructed of brick in an Iraqi style but crowned with a Syrian-inspired gabled roof. Other building complexes were constructed in brick, often elaborately decorated with stucco, some of which have been investigated in recent years. Between 1982 and 1992 important work by Michael Meinecke, tragically interrupted by his untimely death, investigated a number of major complexes located northeast of the city and under imminent threat (Heusch and Meinecke 1985; Meinecke 1991; Heidemann and Becker 2003). These included the Western Palace (110 by 90 metres), divided into ceremonial, living and administrative sections; the North Complex (*c.* 150 by 150 metres), probably the barracks of the imperial guards; the East Complex (*c.* 75 by 50 metres) for recreational use; and the Eastern Palace (*c.* 70 by 40 metres), which was intended for ceremonial purposes.

Like the massive caliphal cities of Baghdad and Samarra in Iraq, al-Raqqah/al-Rafiqah reveals the enormous financial and human resources available to the Abbasids in the later eighth and ninth centuries, but all three foundations were rapidly built using unbaked brick, disguised by the extensive use of stucco panelling decorated with depictions of the Tree of Life (a paradisiacal tree that imparted immortality) and vegetal schemes. With the return of the Abbasid court to Baghdad in 808 these elaborate but hastily built complexes would have soon fallen into decay; like many cities of antiquity, later Raqqah would have presented a mixed urban environment of affluence juxtaposed with decomposition.

In addition to new urban centres, the Umayyad dynasts were vigorous in their establishment of a series of smaller settlements in the more secluded areas of rural Syria-Palestine. Commonly called the 'desert castles' (*qasr / qusur*), even though not all were located in arid zones, probably more has been written on the art and architecture of the *qusur* than on any other topic in early Islamic Syria-Palestine. Debates on the origins and purpose of these enigmatic princely establishments have continued until today, during which time they have been variously interpreted as rural retreats, the nuclei of new agricultural settlements, nodule points on lines of communication, formal meeting points for Umayyad dealings with tribal leaders, and aspirant urban centres for pastoral communities (summarised in Genequand 2006: 3-4; Northedge 2000: 43-54). In general, interpretations have shifted from loose imaginative and misleading 'romantic' causes for their construction to harder economic or social factors (Bacharach 1996; Whitcomb 2001: 506). However, as the body of information on these sites increases through new surveys and excavations, conventional explanations have become less satisfactory and, more confusingly, the boundary between rural estate and new urban foundation increasingly unclear. The diversity of building styles, architecturally and decoratively, can also create uncertainty. No solution seems possible yet, and the diversity of explanations are growing rather than coalescing, but the questions are central to understanding the nature and effectiveness of settlement policies, which were deliberate, structured and extensive, and the process of sedentarisation in early Islamic Syria-Palestine.

In a recent paper, Denis Genequand (2006) has brought considerable clarity to the classification and functional purpose of the Umayyad rural castles, and has highlighted the gradated scale of size and complexity over which they range. The 'classic' type of around 70 metres square had a towered wall pierced with a single gateway only, either flanked by half-round towers or by a split tower. The somewhat awkward split tower gateway seems earlier (for instance at Jabal Says and Qastal), and the dual-towered gateway later (Qasr al-Hayr al-Gharbi and the smaller enclosure at Qasr al-Hayr al-Sharqi), but internally both were laid out with segmented, residential apartments (termed *bayt/buyut*) approached through a common, central courtyard faced with porticoes. While the massive towered walls were inherited from a Roman military tradition and kept for impressive effect, not defence, the internal layout was inspired by local domestic *bayt* architecture, 'but the repetition of the plan and its incorporation into a pseudo-military form is completely new' (Genequand 2006: 25). A second group of castles, often smaller in size, share (with modifications) the towered enclosure wall but internally were uniform and unsegmented until modified by walls inserted within the central court – a result of 'a tension between unifying enclosure and social privacy dramatised in the subsidiary walls subdividing the common court' (Whitcomb 2001: 506). The third group are not so much palaces as large houses, a single residence consisting of rooms around a central court as at Ma'an or the residence of the Abbasid family at Humaymah. As with all classifications, there are those structures that do not fit comfortably into any one of these groupings, such as the early compound of Mu'awiyah at Khirbat al-Karak, which consisted of a large apsidal audience hall, Ghassanid-style, inside a wall with square towers (Whitcomb 2002).

Perplexing in any analysis of the *qusur* is the unfinished and enigmatic *qasr* of Mshatta located 25 kilometres south-south-east of Amman, a huge compound compared with the other castles and noted for its highly decorated façade. First Oleg Grabar (1987) and, more recently, Donald Whitcomb (2001: 507-8) have

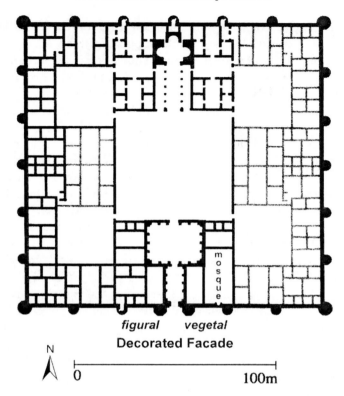

figural   vegetal
Decorated Facade

N

0   100m

Fig. 11. Reconstructed plan of Mshatta (after Genequand 2006: 20,
from a reconstruction by J. Buyard).

expressed serious doubts as to an Umayyad attribution, plumping for an Abbasid origin instead, and by linking its ornamental regime with the famous decorated gateway of the Amman citadel palace have also directly questioned the date of that monument. On Mshatta alone the literature is extensive, and taken with Amman it becomes enormous bordering on staggering, but the debate can be reduced to two interrelated issues: the meaning of the famous façade and the intended function of the entire monument (Fig. 11). Both have direct bearing on establishing a construction date. Neither precludes a late Umayyad one; rather, they would support such an attribution when the fluidity of eighth-century Umayyad art is recognised and, furthermore, the monument is understood as a product of its time.

The perceived difficulties with Mshatta are three-fold: its size, the internal layout (unfinished) and the decorative curtain chosen for the façade (also unfinished). First, size. As noted earlier, the classic type of *qasr* had external dimensions of 70 by 70 metres, whereas Mshatta is a giant square of just over 140 metres each side – obviously merely a doubling of length or quadrupling of area within the towered walls. The same trend to gigantism is likewise apparent in the unfinished Qasr al-Tuba 75 kilometres southeast of Mshatta, which consists of two adjoining compounds each 70 metres square. In both cases the standard Umayyad 70 metre square is adopted as the basic unit, and is simply multiplied. Secondly, the internal layout. There is an unquestionable similarity between Mshatta and the palatial complex on the Amman citadel (and probably the lost example at Baysan; see above), each being a sequential tripartite arrangement of grand entrance, a central walkway flanked by *buyut*, and finally the palace core of triple-apsed throne hall and associated rooms. Again, an Umayyad attribution is not difficult, especially when compared with the greater enclosure at Qasr al-Hayr al-Sharqi. Mshatta represents the application of Qasr al-Hayr al-Sharqi's quasi-urban layout, consisting of a mosque and *buyut* around a central court, to a complex essential palatial in intent; hence, Mshatta is above all a palace dominated by a huge domed throne hall, but also residential, still firmly drawing on Umayyad principles in both cases (Genequand 2006: 18).

The next issue to be considered is the exceptional and enlightening stone carved decoration on the southern façade of the circuit walls. The sumptuous and remarkably eclectic nature of the imagery – seen as inspired by Coptic and Sasanid art simultaneously – has intrigued scholars for over a century, and its inventive individualism within the context of Islamic art in Syria-Palestine has been a major argument put forward in support of a post-Umayyad date. However, the critical mistake has been to evaluate Mshatta in cultural isolation, for in many ways it belongs much more to the last decade of the Umayyads, culturally and politically, than with many other monuments in the preceding decades. As Robert Hillenbrand (1981), Michael Meinecke (1998) and Ghazi Bisheh (1987) show each in their own way, Mshatta in plan and decoration was a product of a rapidly changing age as the centre of gravity of the Islamic world curved eastwards. The façade is a visual testament to an irreversible transition to a new phase in Islamic history that began in the later Umayyad period and culminated in the rise of the Abbasids and the foundation of Baghdad (762-3) and, later, Samarra (836). Thus the cultural gaze of early Islamic Syria-Palestine shifted east a decade or more before the rise of the Abbasids, not solely after. Architecturally and artistically the outcome of this transformation can be seen in the urban expression of Abbasid al-Raqqah, the palace of *c.* 776 at al-Uk-haydir in Iraq, and the enormous palatial compounds of Samarra, the latter a culmination of the trend towards gigantism first seen at Mshatta and with decorative regimes in stucco reminiscent of that monument's façade. Hence the last of the Umayyads commenced what the Abbasids were to complete on an unprecedented scale.

Finally, what was the purpose of Mshatta, with its intended residences and colossal throne room prefixed by a florid façade? Alastair Northedge (2000: 57-8) connects the monument with the hapless caliph al-Walid II and his reception near Jiza, only a few kilometres from Mshatta, of the annual Syrian pilgrimage during its journey back from the Hijaz: 'At a staging-post called Zîzâ' [Jiza] he [al-Walid] would ... feed for a period of three days people returning from the pilgrimage' (Tabari, trans. Hillen-brand 1989: 103-4). Of this there seems little doubt, given the general southern orientation of the complex and, in particular, that of the decorated façade, which confronted the faithful with paradisiacal scenes of an earthly (the Garden of Eden) rather than heavenly quality, resplendent with coiled vine tendrils springing almost river-like from cups and urns interspersed with mythical creatures recalling the fragility of human exist-ence, the certainty of judgement, and the promise of a heavenly paradise through faith; in other words, a reminder of the guar-antee of redemption for the faithful. At least that was the unfulfilled intention of the builder, for the monument was never completed. The decorative regime was abruptly termi-nated and the internal structures, apart from the throne room, were left incomplete. While Walid's monumental ambitions remained unfinished because of his assassination (744), the changing times to which he belonged rushed headlong without him, reaching finality in the architecture of Baghdad, al-Raqqah and, consummately, in the almost immeasurable urban expanse of Samarra (Northedge 2006).

Settlements with intent

Archaeologically, the early Islamic sites of Syria-Palestine, es-pecially under the Umayyads, fit into different settlement cate-gories from those offered in the descriptive geographies of the ninth and tenth centuries (above). Donald Whitcomb (1994a) defines three distinctive groups of sites that developed after the arrival of Islam until the middle of the eighth century, following which natural and human events precipitated site reorganisa-tion. The first group consists of those few sites, notably Damas-cus and Hims, in which a significant number of Muslims occupied abandoned buildings and derelict areas, or acquired houses by other means. Hence in Damascus the construction of the great mosque on the site of the Church of St John could have not been an isolated urban event, but associated with market construction, palace enlargement and house acquisition. In later times Rusafah in north Syria underwent a similar transformation when the caliph Hisham took up residence there, although the palace was built as an independent complex outside the established town (Sack and Becker 1999). Jarash may have been a smaller example of urban intervention, instituted by an unidentified scion of the Umayyad family.

The second group of sites was larger in number, involving the founding of a settlement (Arabic: *misr*, pl. *amsar*) adjacent to an existing town, a principle originating in pre-Islamic times with a *hadir* ('settlement') at places like Aleppo and Qinnasrin. Ramlah, the new capital for Palestine founded by Sulayman, can be viewed as a *misr* set close to Ludd, the probable capital until that date. Aylah in south Jordan was founded right next to the Byzantine town (Whitcomb 1994b), and a *misr* may have been established north of Byzantine Tiberias (Tabariyah). Serving key social and economic functions, these centres were equipped with all the urban fundamentals needed for the times, buildings such as mosque (faith, law, education), palace (administration, justice) and markets (production and trade), laid out to a planned, orthogonal design within prominent circuit walls. These essential urban elements were little changed from the urban ideals of Christian late antiquity as recorded pictorially in church mosaics (above, Chapter 2), but were necessarily adapted to meet the new requirements of a Muslim society.

Whitcomb's third division constitutes dynastic foundations, often associated with landed estates, the showpiece of which was a palace compound. The size, complexity and even purpose of these foundations varied enormously, and many of them were set up under the Umayyads. While Whitcomb does not specify between settlements on the grounds of size or intended function, the distinction is significant. Aspirant towns set in a rural

setting were boldly located within huge walled grounds and
usually came with a mosque, a bath, markets, the provision of
water and a system of waste water disposal. Examples include
Anjar in the Biqa valley of Lebanon (Hillenbrand 1999), Qasr
al-Hayr al-Sharqi in the Syrian steppe, described as a 'city'
(*madinah*) in a lost inscription (Genequand 2004b: 69-88; Grabar et al. 1978), Madinat al-Far on the Khabur River in north
Syria (Haase 1996) and Khirbat al-Mafjar near Jericho (Hamilton 1978, 1988). These presented as a planned palatial
complex, functional yet monumental, equally at home in an
urban context as seen at Amman and Baysan (Almagro and
Arce 2001; Fitzgerald 1931; Northedge 1992; Walmsley f.c.
[2007b]). In all cases the role of the palace was paramount, with
the mosque, markets, bathhouse and water networks as secondary elements. More transitory foundations usually lacked
some and occasionally all of the ancillary buildings, especially
advanced disposal systems for waste. Hence, in spite of its
considerable size, Mshatta's latrines were simple pan and chute
types built into the wall towers, suggesting the intended large-
scale occupation of the complex was only short-term – in effect
a country palace, not a place intended for sizeable permanent
settlement. The disposition and orientation of gates was also
significant; the urban or quasi-urban centres of Anjar and Qasr
al-Hayr al-Sharqi had (like Aylah) four opposing gates centrally
positioned in each wall, whereas palaces such as Mshatta had
one axial gateway opposite the throne room. These features –
plan and utilities – are much more revealing than comparisons
based solely on size.

Whether intended for permanent or intermittent use, 'display' to a local and informed audience was clearly an important
component of the Umayyad foundations, with many being
adorned – sometimes extravagantly – with carved stone decoration, plaster stucco work and paintings depicting human,
animal and vegetal motifs. Except for the mosques, there was

no reluctance to portray human and animal figures. Hence, the painted walls of Qusayr Amra – the little reception hall and bath found by Musil (above, pp. 16-17) – are populated with humans involved in just about every imaginable activity, often scantily and provocatively dressed (recently, Fowden 2004), while the verdant vegetation carved into the south wall of Mshatta sustains an iconographic regime of fantastic animals and the occasional human, but only to the west of the sole axial entrance (Fig. 11). To the gateway's east the decoration was adjusted to present a purely geometric vegetal style, for inside the wall was the complex's mosque, the *qiblah* wall of which with *mihrab* was one and the same as the decorated circuit wall. Remarkable for its variety and eclecticism, the meaning of Umayyad imagery was obviously complicated and many-layered, undoubtedly chosen with clear intent, but probably read in different ways by different observers (Grabar 1993: 96-8).

Rural settlement profiles

As we have seen above, in the early Islamic period the country-side of Syria-Palestine was peppered with many new founda-tions – urban, quasi-urban and rural estates – but what is known of settlement profiles outside these formal estab-lishments, and especially of levels of continuity or discontinuity from late antiquity? Following the enlightening studies of rural sites by, for instance, Howard Butler (1907-49) and particularly Georges Tchalenko (1953-8), the last few decades have been characterised by a rapidly growing interest in mapping and explaining rural settlement patterns in Syria-Palestine (Eddé and Sodini 2005; Foss 1995, 1997; Gatier 2005). Today, few would argue that regional surveys constitute a legitimate area of stand-alone archaeological research in the Middle East. How-ever, much of this work, made all the more urgent by the quickening pace of economic development in the region, has regrettably been too general, often unsystematic and over-ambitious in the geographical area covered. While sometimes permitting gross interpretations of site settlement and land use in the countryside, the results usually lack sufficient precision to allow a more detailed understanding of settlement trends. The outcome has been, in some cases, a somewhat distorted and misleading interpretation of the extent and nature of rural occupation during the later sixth to ninth centuries.

There are three basic problems with much of the survey work undertaken to date, especially that conducted in the south of Syria-Palestine (Walmsley 2005). The first problem is the utter unreliability of surface sherding as an accurate reflection of the underground reality, a general predicament faced by all survey projects but only rarely acknowledged in Syria-Palestine (see, exceptionally, Brown 1991). The second obstacle to valid survey results has been a general absence of reliable ceramic typo-chronologies for much of the region until recently, especially for the transitional later sixth to early eighth centuries. In Jordan, for instance, confusion still reigns as to the correct dating of pottery south of the Wadi Mujib for this period (Johns 1994), with some types being dated anywhere from the mid-sixth to later eighth centuries. Likewise, hand-made wares have conventionally been clumped into the thirteenth to sixteenth centuries, but it is now clear that the first handmade wares appeared in the mid-eleventh century and that they continued after the sixteenth as well. In this way whole historical periods have been overlooked by archaeologists. A third problem is the presentation of survey results in terms of historical periods, and the failure to adjust settlement levels in line with the relative length of each period. Obviously, the archaeological evidence created by three centuries of Byzantine occupation will be considerably greater than that coming from a much shorter 90 Umayyad years, and to compare settlement levels without factoring in this variable is deviously fallacious. Furthermore, there is an assumption that all sites were continuously occupied to their maximum extent for the whole period, but recent archaeological evidence would suggest otherwise. Numerous late antique sites seem to have witnessed a relatively short burst of growth based on localised social and economic factors, and the aspirations of these 'boom villages' – so quickly translated into stone – may have passed very quickly, leaving behind for posterity a visual reminder of the social ambitions harboured by individuals and the community alike. These obstacles to the correct understanding of survey results are now increasingly acknowledged for, as David Graf (2001: 223) recently remarked about south Jordan, survey results 'reflecting rises and declines in Byzantine occupation can only be regarded as impressionistic', with the same holding true for early Islamic Syria-Palestine.

After questioning so intensely the worth of survey results, it may seem a little disingenuous to highlight some of the latest developments in the settlement archaeology of rural areas in Syria-Palestine. Nevertheless, a few noteworthy trends can be seen in this work and these should be at least mentioned, especially as advances in defining ceramic horizons have greatly improved the recognition of Islamic settlement profiles and resource exploitation in the countryside. Properly devised regional surveys have, with little difficulty, identified extensive early Islamic occupation in different environmental zones, for instance the Balikh river valley of north Syria (Bartl 1994, 1996), in the vicinity of Homs (Philip et al. 2002: 19-20, with important observations) and in the Wadi Arabah, where the new settlements were industrial (Avner and Magness 1998). As a result of a programme of detailed area surveys by the Israel Antiquities Authority, major advances have been made in identifying site occupation in the desertous steppe lands of southern Palestine (the Negev/Naqab), and although the settlement interpretations of the survey data vary between scholars the evidence for widespread use of the land is compelling (discussed in Magness 2003). Many of the survey results seem to be supported by the results of recent excavations, such as those in the Balikh valley and the important French work at the village site of Dehes (Dayhis) in the limestone hills between Aleppo and Antioch (Sodini et al. 1980; Tate 1992). Overall, the survey data confirm that many existing sites continued to be occupied without a break and, in some places, new farming and industrial settlements were established, especially in areas adjacent to growing population centres.

However, trends were not entirely consistent, for while the number and size of occupied sites increased in river valleys, there was, by way of contrast, what appears to have been a significant settlement downturn in mountainous areas. Site abandonment apparently occurred early in the hills around Pella (seventh century, Watson and O'Hea 1996), but quite a bit later in the highlands of north Syria (in earnest from the early ninth century, Foss 1997: 197-204; Tate 1992: 275-350). Until now, this settlement shift away from hilly zones has been explained as a result of agricultural changes, the so-called 'green revolution' resulting from the introduction of new crops after Islamic expansion (Watson 1983). However, a new archaeobotanical study on land exploitation in the middle Euphrates valley has raised doubts about any link between the arrival of Islam and the introduction of the new 'revolutionary' crops such as rice and hard wheat, for the evidence indicates that the cultivation of these predates Islam (Samuel 2001). Instead, a growth in rural settlement probably stemmed from the digging of long irrigation canals to supply large elite-owned farm estates and new settlements, a practice known not only from archaeology but also from historical sources. Between 709 and 719 the general Maslamah, son of the caliph Abd al-Malik, commissioned the digging of canals from the Balikh and Euphrates rivers as a financial investment, supplying fields and settlements to increase agricultural productivity and land values (Walmsley 2000: 313-17). Maslamah's rural holdings, while large, were not in any way unusual; many members of the Umayyad family invested in agricultural projects and held their estates until the overthrow of the dynasty, at which time they were confiscated by the Abbasids (Elad 1992). Hence, settlement changes in rural areas after the Islamic expansion resulted from the deliberate development of unproductive land through the building of new infrastructure and only secondarily through the implementation of new agricultural regimes.

The floor of the Jordan Valley offers a very informative example of expanding rural settlement in early Islamic times. In a hot and water-rich zone situated 200 to 400 metres below sea level, a tangible expansion of rural settlement can be seen in the archaeological record. Not only were new estates created, including major holdings of the Umayyad household near Jericho and Tabariyah, numerous agricultural villages also appear on the valley floor between Lake Tiberias and the Dead Sea. Many of these, for instance Tell Abu Qa'dan (Franken and Kalsbeek 1975), were to be continuously occupied for some eight hundred years thereafter.

Site histories and settlement processes

Syria-Palestine in the Early Islamic period was a land of many new opportunities, with a settlement profile ranging from large urban conglomerates to secondary towns and villages in the surrounding countryside. The political, administrative and, especially, economic policies of the Umayyads maintained and promoted, by way of princely and local patronage, the infrastructure of many existing towns, if unequally at times. These policies found expression in the construction of mosques and administrative centres as well as the development of commercial facilities. In some instances the urban network was embellished by the establishment of new centres at strategic points, notably Anjar, Ramlah and Aylah. As in earlier historical periods, the policies of the Umayyads resulted in urban 'winners' and 'losers', if that is the right way to view it; hence, the rise of Tabariyah to the detriment of Baysan, Hims in place of Apamea, and Qinnasrin (but ultimately Aleppo) instead of Antioch. While there were significant changes, overall urban life continued strongly in early Islamic Syria-Palestine.

In rural areas a major investment in agricultural projects, the exploitation of natural resources and setting up of new industrial projects resulted in the establishment of many new settlements, but perhaps at the expense of neighbouring marginal zones. Geomorphological and palaeobotanical studies suggest that the elevated regions of Syria-Palestine experienced increasingly severe erosion and degradation of soil quality from the sixth century onwards, seemingly the result of accelerating deforestation and intensive land use (Bintliff 2002 and below, Chapter 5). Simultaneously, climate change may have exacerbated declining levels of soil fertility in the hills (Lucke et al. 2005). Before long underemployed highland farmers were to follow in the track of the soil to the valley floors and there, often under a Muslim patron, establish new places to live. The social repercussions of these changes on rural settlement profiles were, ultimately, both profound and permanent. Coinciding with significant changes to the pattern and character of urban settlement, as noted earlier in this chapter, the movement of a sizeable segment of the population to new, economically successful locations – both urban and rural – would have contributed to the gradual, probably inadvertent, breakdown of the old social order of late antiquity. The result was the emergence of a new, refashioned society in ninth-century Syria-Palestine, a society still deeply appreciative of its multilayered cultural inheritance yet increasingly ready to embrace Islam and, even more widely, communicate in Arabic.

5

Life

Identifying life processes through the reconstruction of extinct
societal norms and practices has become a standard part of
archaeology since the groundbreaking impact of 'new archaeology' in the 1960s. Although these changes have generally been
slow to catch on in the Middle East, Islamic archaeology has
been less reticent than other archaeologies in attempting to
reconstruct and interpret past ways of life. This chapter looks
at the field from five aspects: the acquisition and preparation of
food; the place of industry and trade; religious life; housing and
domestic life; and lastly the environment and landscape. Although much needs to be done, and such objectives need to be
fully integrated into current and new projects, we know considerably more, and interpret results better, than a mere thirty
years ago.

Food

Given the proposed agricultural 'revolution' that coincided,
approximately, with the arrival of Islam in Syria-Palestine, it
is something of a surprise and an even greater disappointment
that Islamic archaeology has paid little attention to integrating
archaeobotanical studies more fully in excavation projects. Archaeozoological material, especially smaller species (birds,
fish), has been similarly overlooked. Collecting ecofacts profes-
sionally and systematically by sieving and flotation is the exception, rather than the norm, on most (but not solely) Islamic

113

projects, yet when undertaken the analysis of the data has produced interesting results. The issue is particularly significant for Islamic archaeology. The identification, from literature and archaeologically, of the intensification of irrigation regimes dating to the eighth century has indicated significant changes in practices in Umayyad times, but only archaeobotanical data can accurately document cultivation techniques by identifying weed varieties harvested accidentally with the principal food crops, for instance wheat or barely (see, for an excellent example from Jordan, Charles and Hoppé 2003). The Jordan study reveals that 'fields under different water regimes have different weed floras' (Charles and Hoppé 2003: 228) – in other words, grain crops grown seasonally under irrigation will be associated with different weeds than those produced in fields watered solely by rain. A second science-based method can also assist in reliably identifying crops grown under irrigation, involving an analysis of solid deposits of silica called phytoliths found in plant remains such as cereal husks (Rosen 1999; Rosen and Weiner 1994). Phytoliths are particularly suitable for analysis because of their high durability in the archaeological record, relative ease of recovery and the demonstrated linkage between the size and complexity of phytoliths to cultivation techniques. The microscopic examination of cultivated plant remains can distinguish between the smaller-sized phytoliths deposited in dry-farmed crops and the larger, multi-celled phytoliths formed in irrigated crops, with most experimentation being done on grain cultivates to date, especially wheat and barley. As analytical techniques such as these are more widely applied, they promise to document whether irrigation projects were indeed the primary factor in rural development in the early Islamic period, rather than solely crop introductions, and resolve the important and, as yet, unanswered question whether irrigation was used only for commercial crops or applied more generally in early Islamic Syria-Palestine.

114

Archaeobotanical samples recovered from Umayyad levels at a few sites in Syria-Palestine have helped to establish the basic diet of the period, which was based on local grains, nuts and fruit. Umayyad levels at Pella produced club wheat, two-rowed hulled barley (not usually irrigated), and, for the first time, six-rowed hulled barley (possibly irrigated), as well as pistachio (Willcox 1992: 256). Busra produced two-rowed barley, free-threshing wheat (*triticum*), lentil and grass pea in addition to the common Mediterranean fruits of fig, olive and grape (Samuel 1986). The Cornelian cherry was also found at Busra, usable as a food (in drinks and sweets) and in medicine. At Rusafah, two-rowed barley, olive, grape, onion and leek, almond and fat hen were recovered, all dry-tolerant species (von Willerding 1984). Of these the last is a weedy vegetable common on freshly cultivated land, probably self-sowing but tolerated in that, apart from an edible leaf also usable as chicken feed, it produces nutritious seeds. On the middle Euphrates, the cutting of a canal allowed the cultivation of hard wheat (durum), cotton, rice, millet and sesame, spreading further improvements that predated the arrival of Islam (Samuel 2001).

The archaeozoological evidence shows little deviation from an earlier, pre-Islamic reliance on sheep, goat, cattle and camel for milk, meat, wool, bone and leather. Chickens were also important for eggs and meat, while dove and fish bone were additionally recovered. At Pella, domesticated pig was also prevalent in Umayyad levels but rarer in the Abbasid deposits excavated off the main tell (and hence free from contamination by earlier material: see the archaeozoological report by Kevin Reilly in Walmsley et al. 1993: 218-21), which would seem to indicate a significant dietary shift in the eighth century. Other animals identified at Pella were small equid (mostly mule/donkey), dog, cat, large deer and rodents, the latter probably post-occupation intrusive. The eighth-ninth century village site of Elat-Elot near Aqabah produced predominantly goat/sheep, camel (some bones with slaughter marks) and fish bones. The faunal assemblage of other Naqab sites was likewise dominated by sheep/goat bone (Horwitz 1998), a reflection of the environmental severity of the region. A detailed study of the faunal remains from the houses at Apamea has isolated a wide range of mammals, fish and birds, both wild and domesticated (Gautier 1984). In addition to chickens, ducks, pigeons and geese constituted many of the bird bones. Identified trends from the early seventh century include a reduction in fish and pig bone numbers, the latter similar to changes at Pella, and a greater reliance on goat, which, it was argued, reflected the ruralisation/nomadisation of Apamea. However, other explanations are just as possible such as the degradation of pastoral lands and/or the evacuation of hilly agriculture fields in favour of the well-watered floor of the nearby Orontes Valley – factors of change already proposed earlier in this book.

How much agriculture and the production of food had changed in Syria-Palestine by the tenth century is apparent from the Arab geographies composed in that century (Chapter 4). Two writers are especially informative: Ibn Hawqal (d. *c.* 988) and al-Maqdisi (d. 1000), both of whom travelled widely to collect first-hand information (their books are available in translation: Ibn Hawqal trans. Kramers and Weit 1964; Muqaddasi (al-Maqdisi) trans. Collins 1994). Both feature the interesting and unusual goods for which the towns and districts of the Islamic world were especially known. New crops included sugar cane, grown for instance near coastal Bayrut and Akka as well as Tabariyah in the Jordan Valley, rice at Baysan, bananas at Jericho, the lotus and lemons. Also grown on a commercial scale was indigo at Jericho and on the hot plain south of the Dead Sea. Here two trends can be observed: the commercial production of crops beyond subsistence and the adoption of new, exotic varieties that catered to changing urban tastes in the Islamic world, sugar in particular.

Industry

The crowding of town centres with shops and markets in the late antique/early Islamic transition (above, Chapter 2) was concurrent with the expansive, almost explosive, growth of industrial activity within towns and in their immediate hinterlands. The archaeological evidence uncovered in the last few decades is extensive and almost overwhelming in volume and diversity (Foote 1999; 2000; Walmsley 2000: 305-10). Ceramic factories, glassblowing workshops, metalworking centres, tanneries and textile mills occupied vacated spaces such as abandoned temples or culturally and functionally obsolete Roman-period bathhouses in towns throughout Syria-Palestine. Being concrete and large-scale activities, these industries are well represented in the archaeological record, but almost certainly other less tangible trades such as woodworking or bone carving would also have flourished alongside the high-waste manufacturing industries.

Evidence for the commercial production of ceramics resulting from a significant investment of money and resources has been recovered from Umayyad levels in the two towns of Baysan and Jarash. At Baysan, preparation areas, a storeroom and ten updraft kilns were uncovered around the derelict Roman-period theatre (Tsafrir and Foerster 1997: 137). Pipes and channels fed water to the factory, which produced a large range of domestic vessels and lamps. Great quantities of wasters, lamp moulds and unbaked pottery were recovered, while two kilns were found with their contents still intact. Kilns and related installations were also found in other parts of the town, demonstrating the extent of pottery manufacture in early Islamic Baysan. Across the Jordan at Jarash, pottery manufacture was also practised on a commercial scale, especially at the deserted North Theatre and, on an even larger scale, in the forecourt of the dilapidated Temple of Artemis (Pierobon 1983-4;

Schaefer and Falkner 1986). Further south at Aylah, excavations uncovered a group of industrial-size kilns used in the large-scale manufacture of pottery amphorae for shipping of goods by sea, as well as cooking pots, casseroles and water juglets for local consumption (Melkawi et al. 1994).

The active potting sector of urban economies continued unabated into Abbasid times (ninth century). At Jarash, three kilns producing cooking pots, moulded lamps, 'cut' bowls and Red Painted cups were placed within a commercial complex located on the south cross-street, while potters' workshops have also been uncovered at al-Ramlah, Tabariyah, and Caesarea. The Caesarea kilns, of Abbasid-Tulunid date (ninth century), produced lamps and decorated Cream ware bowls, cups and water bottles (Holum and Hohlfelder 1988: 231-41). Raqqah was, likewise, the host to a large ceramics industry in Abbasid times, as well as in later periods (Heidemann 2006; Meinecke 1995).

Other prominent industrial activities in early Islamic Syria-Palestine included glassblowing, which utilised the extensive sand formations along the Mediterranean coast, and textile manufacture based on flax and, increasingly, cotton cultivation.

Glassmaking is identifiable from crucibles, raw glass chunks and waste in addition to the finished products. A series of furnaces for the preparation of raw glass dating to the sixth to ninth centuries has been identified on the coast of Palestine, including a huge nine-ton slab abandoned because the glass failed to fuse properly (Freestone, Gorin-Rosen and Hughs 2000; Goren-Rosen 2000: 52-6). Reprocessing the raw glass chunks into vessels had a wider geographical distribution, often being located away from the coast where fuel was readily available. Industrial debris has been recovered from a number of major towns, including Raqqah, Caesarea, Dor, Arsuf, Ramlah, Jarash and Pella, indicating that the manufacture of glass vessels took place at most major centres (Dussart 1998; Henderson 1999).

For textile preparation, defunct bathhouses offered a particularly suitable location, as the manufacturing and dying process both required large volumes of water. At Baysan, noted for its flax cultivation in the geographical sources, the domed hall of the eastern bath was subdivided into four rooms around a central court, with six pools and a plastered workspace in each room. Channels fed water into the pools and drains let waste water out. Similar workshops probably involved in textile weaving and dyeing have been found at Tabariyah and, recently, in the south tetrakionia plaza bathhouse and the huge east baths at Jarash.

By the ninth century, the establishment of industrial quarters dedicated to the production of high-grade tradable commodities became a standard feature of urban life in Syria-Palestine. The trend to urban industrialisation had unquestionably begun long before, in late antiquity, but speeded up and reached a spectacular culmination in early Islamic times owing to the increasing demands of a moneyed middle socio-economic group and the presence of local notables willing to invest in profitable projects. Requiring considerable investment and constructed on a large scale, many of these industries came to be located on the outer edge of towns because of their polluting and potentially dangerous nature. The vast field of industrial waste from glass and pottery manufacture on the outskirts of Raqqah is the clearest example of this phenomenon (Heidemann 2006; Henderson 1999; Meinecke 1995).

The industrialisation of economic activity in early Islamic Syria-Palestine reached outside the confines of urban centres into the wider countryside. In addition to the processing of primary products and resource exploitation characteristic of pre-Islamic times, new industrial activities designed to feed growing urban centres were established near suitable natural resources with a day's journey of towns. In a recent study, Uzi Avner and Jodi Magness (1998) have drawn together previously unrelated archaeological discoveries from the southern Arabah and al-Naqab to detail higher levels of mineral ore exploitation and smelting in the rural hinterland of Aylah. Copper was mined at several locations, with one mine having galleries and halls over three kilometres long. Smelting camps were established by the mines, being easily identified by expanses of slag waste from the smelting process. Acacia was the preferred wood for the charcoal used in smelting the copper ore. Evidence for gold production and a stone quarry was also found. Six villages were coupled to the mining and smelting activities, and their uniform characteristics and standard room dimensions suggest that these villages were created at the direction of a single body, presumably one composed of local notables. Each village had an industrial basis for its economy, notably copper smelting, pottery firing or shell working for jewellery and furniture inlays. Associated with this development was the construction of an irrigated agricultural estate and fortress at the oasis of Ghadhian (Yotvata), from which was recovered a gold dinar from the reign of the Abbasid caliph al-Mahdi (775-785), indicating continued importance of the south Arabah until the end of the eighth century, if not later. The archaeological evidence from the Aylah hinterland is impressive but surely not exceptional for eighth-century Syria-Palestine, in that the countryside around many towns would have supported a range of mining and industrial activities depending on local needs and resources. The data indicate that these capital intensive industries were coordinated and promoted in accordance with a standardised plan by wealthy and influential groups in early Islamic Syria-Palestine.

Religious life

... the cultural and political change brought about by the Muslim conquest did not result in an immediate change in the life of the Palestinian Christians: until the late eighth century at least, they did not convert en masse to Islam, and the communities continued to cater to their religious needs by restoring their religious buildings and erecting others whenever necessary (Di Segni 2003: 257).

The arrival and consolidation of Islam as a creed at the start of the seventh century added another layer to an already rich religious history in late antique Syria-Palestine. Although the region was overwhelmingly Christian by the end of the sixth century, as attested by its many known churches (see especially Ovadiah 1970, 1993; Piccirillo 1993), a sizeable Jewish community also existed, centred on Galilee and the Jawlan with Tiberias as a major seat of learning and religious life. To these communities was added a third important group, the Muslims, yet numbers remained small – perhaps very small – for a long period after the expansion of Islam into Syria-Palestine. Frustratingly, archaeology has contributed little to comprehending the development of Muslim life (except that of elites) in the seventh and eighth centuries (Hoyland 2006; Johns 2003), and until now most attention has been paid to comprehending from an archaeological perspective the condition and survival of Christian and Jewish communities in Syria-Palestine after Islam.

A major issue that has continued to captivate scholars of late antiquity is the question of iconoclasm – the destruction of images of humans and animals in churches and synagogues. A 'fear of images' (iconophobia) in sacred places preoccupied much of the Middle East in the eighth and ninth centuries – Christian, Muslim and Jewish – although the dislike of images had existed long before. As mentioned earlier (Chapter 1), the discovery of iconoclastic damage to church mosaics in the mid-twentieth century was frequently attributed to Muslim persecution, in which Jews were also seen as complicit. Hence at Jarash, 'all representations of living creatures were ruthlessly destroyed'

in the churches (Kraeling 1938: 69), such as those once inhab-
iting the floor mosaics in the nave of Jarash's Synagogue
Church and 'presumably ... mutilated by the adherents of a
third religion', a somewhat apathetic reference to Muslims
(Crowfoot 1938: 239). Conversely, the iconoclastic disfigurement of images in synagogues was blamed on Christian and
Muslim fanatics. More recent, and reasoned, studies on the
mosaic evidence in churches and synagogues have questioned
many of these suppositions, especially given the considerable
care often devoted to the repair of image-purged mosaic floors.
Attention has turned to a consideration of changing attitudes
by indigenous Christians and Jews towards their own places of
prayer, either as a largely autonomous movement within each
faith group or, perhaps, as an adaptive measure in which
Muslim views opposed to the depiction of living things in holy
places were partly absorbed and adapted (Bowersock 2006:
91-111; Fine 2000; Schick 1995: 213-19). Unlike in the mid-
twentieth century, evidence for radical iconoclasm is no longer
decoded as an instrument of socio-political oppression wielded
tyrannically by any one religious group over another; rather, it
was an internal movement with its own supporters and distrac-
ters within each faith, often with demonstrable differences of
opinion right down to a local level.

The identification and excavation of numerous synagogues
in towns and in rural areas, the latter commonly associated
with agricultural villages, has thoroughly documented the nature and extent of the Jewish community in southern
Syria-Palestine, with central and eastern Galilee being pre-
dominately Jewish until the sixth century (Levine 1982; Urman
and Flesher 1995: 373-617). However, the archaeological evidence indicates that many synagogues, especially in the
countryside, had fallen out of use by the mid-sixth century, such
as at Khirbat Shema (destroyed by earthquake in the early to
mid-fifth century) and Meiron (abandoned mid-fourth century).

Of interest is the conversion of a synagogue into a church in 530-1 at Jarash, in which the orientation of the building was altered 180 degrees and new floor mosaics laid over the original pictorial mosaics of the synagogue, which depicted the Biblical Flood and a menorah among other things (Kraeling 1938: 234-41, 473). As these mosaics reveal no evidence of deliberate disfigurement, most notably to a dedicatory inscription in Aramaic written in Hebrew characters, the alterations to the building seem to represent the conversion of a local Jewish population, not usurpation (contra Wharton 2000: 202-6). While proclaiming their new religious outlook by changing their synagogue into a church, the converted Jews of Jarash took care to preserve a long-standing congregational (and tribal?) memory by concealing, rather than obliterating, the material manifestation of a communal past.

While there had been a reduction in the total number of synagogues in use by the middle of the sixth century due to interacting cultural, religious and economic causes, a good number of synagogues continued to function into the early seventh century and, as with churches, passed seamlessly into the early Islamic period thereafter. Found all over Palestine, northern examples include the synagogues at Hammat Tabariyah (Dothan and Johnson 2002) and Merot, the later continuing into the twelfth century (Ilan 1989) and, in the south, those at Jericho and Khirbat Susiyah. The latter synagogue, located 60 kilometres south of Jerusalem, continued in use until the eighth or ninth century, during which time images on the marble panels were erased. Hence the archaeological evidence from synagogues, as with churches, has consistently shown that the change from a Byzantine Christian to Muslim ruling authority in Syria-Palestine had little negative impact on Jewish and Christian religious life, either in the short or the medium term.

Rather than just surviving, however, Christian and Jewish

communities in Syria-Palestine regularly managed to do significantly better by adapting positively to the new circumstances they faced following the arrival of Islam, as recent archaeological and architectural studies have strongly indicated. Indeed, these studies reveal that religious life continued to flourish as seen in the embellishment of existing religious buildings and the ongoing construction of new ones. As Leah Di Segni (2003: 247), for example, remarks: 'Christian life went on on both sides of the Jordan, not as an ebbing survival, but as the expression of a flourishing, self-assured and self-organised community.' A similar view has been expressed from an historical perspective by Ahmad Shboul (Shboul and Walmsley 1998: 269-70). Rather than enervating Christian society, the establishment of Islamic Arab rule in Syria-Palestine served to strengthen Christian communities and their leaders as they responded to new challenges and opportunities, encouraging them to become increasingly self-reliant, reinforcing self-identity and building a new cultural orientation, the latter especially seen in the adoption of Arabic by the Church.

In this light, recent archaeological discoveries showing continued care of a religious infrastructure should not be viewed as either exceptional or unexpected. In the area of modern Jordan, work headed by Michele Piccirillo of the Franciscan Archaeological Institute has documented extensive church activity in early Islamic times, especially the eighth century (Piccirillo 1984; Piccirillo and Alliata 1994). For example, at Umm al-Rasas (Kastron Mefaa) near Madaba, enormous effort was put into adorning the impressive Church of St Stephen with an expansive mosaic carpet in 718, on which the many towns of the Holy Land were individually depicted in, contrastingly, a spiritual unity – a 'family of cathedral churches' with which the Christian community of Umm al-Rasas longingly sought company. Refurbished later in the same century (in 756), St Stephen's is one of a number of eighth-century mosaics found in the Madaba district, such as at the florid Church of the Virgin at Madaba, and elsewhere in Jordan, for instance the al-Quwaysmah church in Amman dated to 717-18 and the acropolis church at Ma'in of 719/20 (Michel 2001). As a group, the eighth-century church mosaics in Jordan do not show any trend to abstraction, with both figurative and geometric decorative programmes continuing from established Byzantine traditions. If anything, a tendency to 'naturalism of the classical tradition' (Piccirillo 1993: 36) can be observed in the mosaic images, as symmetry gave way to greater realism.

The portrait of an equally active church life for Palestine in the early Islamic period has been convincingly depicted by Leah Di Segni (2003) based on recent archaeological evidence, especially epigraphic sources. Acknowledging the overwhelming proof for a continuation of Christian communities in Jordan, Di Segni lays out the increasingly large body of evidence for Palestine: a Church of St George (762) and a chapel dedicated to the Holy Martyrs (probably 701), both near Jerusalem, and the refurbishment in the later eighth or early ninth century of the Cathisma Church of the Virgin Mary, located between Jerusalem and Bethlehem, with a new mosaic and the introduction of a mihrab, after which the building was jointly used by both Christians and Muslims. On the other side of Jerusalem a monastery, situated on the Jericho road, was luxuriously expanded with guest rooms and a bathhouse in the eighth century. Away from Jerusalem, in which a continuing high level of activity may have been expected given its importance to Christians, the evidence is just as compelling: a new mosaic floor at Jabaliyah near Gaza (732), a new church with mosaics at the village of Aristobulias near Hebron (701), a new mosaic for the church at Khirbat Yattir (perhaps 725), and from Galilee repairs and enlargement to a village church, to which was joined a monastery, dated by an inscription to either 785/6 or 801/2 (depending on the relevant era). Three further phases were identified in the life of the church, with archaeological evidence suggesting that occupation continued into the tenth century. Such a date is quite probable, given the demonstrably long history for the churches and synagogues of Tiberias (Dothan and Johnson 2000; Hirschfeld 2004b: 75-134) and elsewhere. As Di Segni concludes in her important paper (2003: 257-8):

... when dating Christian buildings lacking objective chronological data – e.g., layers associated with coins, or a dated inscription – the archaeologist can no longer adopt the Muslim conquest as a *terminus post quem non*. At the present state of research, this widespread presumption is no longer valid. The same must be said for the epigraphist. Greek inscriptions in churches must not necessarily be earlier than the mid-seventh century. It is imperative to revise the dating of inscriptions lacking explicit chronological data or valid archaeological dating arguments, with the help of palaeography.

Housing and domestic life

Middle Eastern archaeology is not alone in spending little time investigating domestic areas of archaeological sites. Traditionally, the focus of work has been on major public monuments, especially religious or palatial edifices, so as to reveal the past grandeur of a 'lost' civilisation, or to illuminate early Christianity through architecture and art history. Moreover later phases of occupation and changed use of space in buildings after antiquity have often been summarily dismissed, branded as 'squatter' and therefore irrelevant. Islamic sites in Syria-Palestine have often been treated in a similarly cursory manner, yet the importance and worth of digging domestic units is not unappreciated by Islamic archaeologists. The interest in housing quarters is seen as particularly relevant for contemporary research into social continuity and change, for domestic sites preserve ways of life lived by everyday people, rather than a fabricated public show constructed by the nobility. For the early Islamic period two types of houses are discernable: those places built in pre-Islamic times that are used continually into the Islamic period, and secondly new housing units designed and built for evolving urban and rural realities after the arrival of Islam.

The development of houses as an organic, living social institution within towns during the late antique/early Islamic transition can be observed in a number of excavations in Syria-Palestine, including Apamea (Balty 1984; Foss 1997: 217-26) and Pella (recent reassessment in Walmsley f.c. [2007a]). At Apamea, the grand two-storey residences of late Roman date, often resplendent with floor mosaics, painted stucco and marble panelling, underwent a common process typified by the internal subdivision of space through the construction of dividing walls and changed activities – industrial, agricultural processing, domestic and animal stabling – within the house. In short, between the fourth and tenth centuries the houses changed in progressive stages from prestigious mansions – symbols of a socially condoned and expected urban pride – to everyday living quarters in which mixed economic activities were undertaken.

It is easy to be judgemental about the nature of these changes. Clive Foss uses terms such as 'deteriorated' and 'chaotic', but to say 'the old order had broken down, and the house was occupied in a completely different way by a different kind of people' (Foss 1997: 218) complies too comfortably with the interpretations offered by the excavators, who argue for occupational discontinuity at Apamea and social displacement, characterised by the 'ruralisation' of the urban environment and typical of the whole Roman east in the sixth to eighth centuries (Balty 1984: 497-8). There is no question that after several hundred years and a succession of pillages, earthquakes

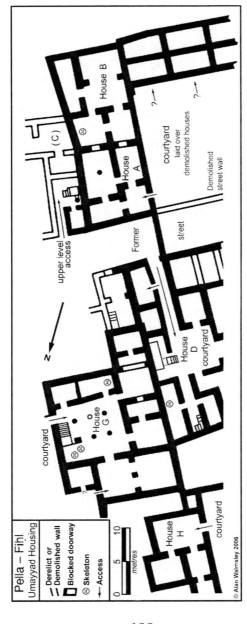

Fig. 12. General plan of the domestic units at Pella, destroyed in the 749 CE earthquake (Walmsley).

and fires, the houses of unfortunate Apamea had lost their former glory, in that their urban role had changed from components in a regime of elaborate social display befitting the nobility of a provincial capital to practical living units. Yet life in these homes is probably better characterised as 'lively' than 'chaotic', an indication of ongoing economic vigour coinciding with shifting social perspectives. Internal space was subdivided and functionally redefined, the ground floor being applied to practical uses for the generation of wealth, rather than for an ostentatious and increasingly unappreciated display of family wealth. This is another way of seeing change; whether it represents decline is simply a question of opinion depending on the starting point.

The gap between perception and reconstructed reality in interpreting living standards in early Islamic towns has been graphically demonstrated by the excavations of a domestic quarter at the eastern end of the main mound at Pella (Fig. 12). Excavations in the early 1980s identified six house units destroyed in the earthquake of 749. These houses represented the last phase in a long urban development that commenced with the complete redevelopment of living quarters on Pella's main mound in the first half of the sixth century (Watson 1992). The original arrangement consisted of four-metre wide gravelled streets set out on a formal grid, each street flanked by stone and mudbrick terrace-style houses two storeys high, prefaced in some places by shops. These streets, intended to serve local needs, were not equipped with colonnades or sidewalks. Although modified, the layout remained the same until an earthquake in 659-60 required a rebuilding of the quarter, in which the linear terrace houses were replaced by independent, self-contained units centred on one or more sizeable courtyards. Six of these courtyard houses, all completely destroyed in the 749 earthquake, were excavated. Each house was probably two-storeyed with well-built double-faced stone walls over a metre thick on the ground floor and an upper floor of unbaked yellow-clay bricks. In some cases upper floors were paved with plain mosaic over a pebble and mortar base, the walls plastered and painted (red, yellow, cream and fragments of text in black), and fitted out with fixtures in stone, often re-used marble some of which clearly came from a church. Roofs were flat and not tiled. Commonly, the upper floors were reached by staircases located in the courtyards, indicating that courtyard space was understood as belonging to the house and its inhabitants, rather than serving any community role.

One house is especially revealing as to living standards and available wealth at Pella in the middle of the eighth century. Household G stood at the eastern end of the main mound, with an orientation to the east. In plan the house consisted of a central paved courtyard with flanking rooms on three sides, and a broad staircase on the east side which gave access to the upper floor. The upstairs rooms opened out onto a balcony, which was supported by six columns in the courtyard. The excavation of Household G recovered a wide range of finds on two levels, including from the destroyed upper floor numerous domestic items such as locally-made unglazed ceramic vessels and lamps, copper objects, blown glass vessels with ribbon trailing, bone buttons, inlay from wood furniture, and stone items including a basalt hand mill for grains. Entombed on the ground floor level were more domestic goods along with many victims of the tragedy, human and animal. The human victims consisted of three adults; a single male in Room 2 and a couple under the staircase in the central courtyard. With these were found their portable wealth in gold coinage, in total the quite considerable amount of ten dinars. Wealth was also evident in the silk clothing of the couple, carbonised in a subsequent fire (Eastwood 1992). The animals on the ground floor were chiefly cows (Rooms 8 and 9, totalling three) and small equids (mules or donkeys; inner courtyard and Rooms 6 and 7) – more costly animals than sheep and goats, hence their owners' wish to shelter them properly during winter, the season in which the earthquake struck. Based on the disposition of the artefacts in the collapse and the complete entrapped skeletons on the ground floor, it can be generalised that the downstairs area of the house focused on the central internal courtyard where much of the daily life of the household took place, including cooking, the care of valuable domesticated animals and, in one corner (Room 3), light craft activities. The primary living quarters were located upstairs, and these were comfortably, although not luxuriously, furnished.

Evidence from the other houses at Pella reveals a comparable winter domestic arrangement involving mixed activities including animal stabling, workshop production, storage of goods and some aspects of daily living (cooking and perhaps transit accommodation) at ground floor level, whereas much of the social life of the household occurred in the rooms of the upper floor. Access to the upstairs living quarters was by a staircase that could be reached only through a private courtyard. Between the mid-seventh and mid-eighth century, the most significant difference in domestic arrangements was in the disposition of the houses, from continuous terrace-style to independent units centred on open courtyards. This change in urban planning was part of a greater focalisation of activities in the towns of Syria-Palestine across all spheres: domestic, commercial and religious. The beginnings of these changes predated Islam, and therefore document a society already in transformation of which Islam was at first a part and then, later, a contributor.

One interesting dimension in the study of housing styles in eighth-century Syria-Palestine is the apparent convergence of urban house plans to those seen in rural settings, especially the Hawran and the Negev, during the sixth and seventh centuries, which has often been interpreted as a component in the proposed 'ruralisation' of the urban environment. Looking at the plan of the house units at Umm al-Jimal (Knauf 1984; de Vries 1998), Subaytah (Sobata; Hirschfeld 2003) and Msayké (Guérin 1997), for instance, there are many shared details that differ noticeably from the 'terrace-style' street houses of antiquity: the prominence of a central private courtyard flanked by rooms used for a variety of functions, with upstairs living quarters reached only by a courtyard staircase. These houses were spacious, intentionally capable of supporting an extended family and its various economic activities. The adoption of this housing, remarkably uniform in plan and area though not without evidence of social stratification, in an urban context would seem to reflect changing socio-economic expectations of family life that were independent of religious affiliation, for at Pella the trend is both apparent before the arrival of Islam and continued in a town that was never overtly Islamic in the lead up to the terrible destruction by earthquake in 749. The change, then, was not a symptom of urban failure but, rather, a deliberate shift towards an all-encompassing house unit suited to the multifaceted socio-economic activities of households in the towns of early Islamic Syria-Palestine. These changes further blurred the division of village from town, structurally and culturally, first apparent in the surge of rural construction that typified late antiquity (above, Chapter 2).

Environment, landscape and
the human factor

Issues of climate change and environmental catastrophe have swiftly gained greater prevalence in archaeological studies during the last decade as the modern world faces these major challenges to our own lifestyle. The depletion of water resources in the Middle East in recent times has given the question even greater relevance (Enzel et al. 2003: 271-2). More rain, less rain, land degradation and the over-exploitation of natural resources have been posited as causal factors behind historical change during the late antique/early Islamic transitional period, often deterministically, but to date no consensus has been reached while much of the available data is scientifically deficient.

The question of more advantageous climatic conditions in late antiquity has featured widely in archaeological literature since the exploration of marginal settlements in the desertous fringes of southern Palestine and eastern Jordan and Syria (reviewed for the Negev in Magness 2003: 78). As noted earlier, these sites underwent a major, almost environmentally disproportionate, expansion in the sixth and seventh centuries, a phenomenon readily attributed by some writers to moister environmental conditions between the fourth to sixth centuries allowing greater agricultural productivity in marginal zones (recently, using palaeoclimatic and archaeological data, Hirschfeld 2004a). Likewise dryer conditions, it has been argued, had an adverse effect on human society, potentially resulting in dramatic cultural and political collapse. Hence, recently, Yehouda Enzel et al. (2003: 268), using Dead Sea level data, have drawn a direct link between an environmental desiccation of the late fifth to late eighth century and the proposed collapse of Byzantine-period agriculture and the 'Arab expansion' into Syria-Palestine from the Arabia Peninsula, confirming in their view a 'synchronism between cultural changes and climate impact in the Near East'. Even the most causal observer will immediately see an obvious inconsistency in the two climatic views of Hirschfeld and Enzel et al., with both data and interpretation irreconcilable. While Hirschfeld argues for significant improvement in the crucial sixth century, Enzel et al. propose collapse. Furthermore, different causal agents can be proposed; for example, suggested falling lake levels after the sixth century might have resulted from more water being drawn out of the Jordan River system for irrigation (above), and not from less precipitation. Then again, another recent study based on soil sedimentation in highland north Jordan has argued for drought over one hundred years in the later Abbasid period, leading to the depopulation of the region where fragile soils were particularly susceptible to dry spells (Lucke et al. 2005: esp. 78-9). All rather confusing, actually, but the problem may be more imagined than real, for a contrary position has been also argued: that there has been no significant change in the climate in the last two millennia and, therefore, other causes for change must be sought (Rubin 1989). Attention has turned increasingly to identifying and measuring human influences on the natural environment, especially the impact of land use – and particularly misuse – on urban and rural landscapes.

In Claudio Vita-Finzi's pioneering study of the 1960s (Vita-Finzi 1969), an explanation for the rapid infilling of valleys in the east Mediterranean, known as 'the Younger Fill', focused on a number of largely human factors, specifically overgrazing, excessive tree-felling and the failure, probably from neglect, of agricultural terraces, although the question of climate change was also entertained (Vita-Finzi 1969: 83-8, 101-2). Subsequent evidence has tended to weigh in favour of the importance of human impact on the landscape, in which a direct link between soil erosion and intensive agriculture has been argued, although reasoning has tended to be simplistic, circular and self-fulfilling (Bintliff 2002; conceptually important is Butzer 2005). Unfortunately, unlike elsewhere in the Mediterranean, most evidence from Syria-Palestine has, until recently, been incidental and not the result of interdisciplinary research programmes in regional geoarchaeology, which seriously questions its worth.

Nevertheless, at Pella there is clear proof for substantial infilling of the central valley after antiquity. Erosional deposits many metres deep overlie the 'downtown' area of the Roman town, which consisted of a colonnaded decumanus and a forum or market, known only from an image preserved on a city coin of Commodus (r. 177-92) minted in 183-4. Recent deep digging in the valley to extract water confirms the extent of the infilling. Excavation of a church on the edge of the valley showed that the influx of erosional deposits became an impossible problem in the later sixth to early seventh century, ending the useful life of the odeum, baths and lower Roman-period town (Smith and Day 1989: 8, 18, 29, 90). Similar problems of wash deposits invading urban centres have been identified at other sites, including Jarash, Baysan and Bayt Ras, where urban infrastructure became rapidly and permanently engulfed in gravelly washes from the fourth and fifth centuries onwards. At Baysan, street levels in the lower town were raised as an alternative to keeping existing surfaces clear, while at Jarash gravelled surfaces were laid over the buried north decumanus.

The environmental breakdown of the landscape around towns may be attributable to an overexploitation of soils in the area, the progressive vacating of farmlands on the lower valley slopes (for the Pella hinterland, see Watson and O'Hea 1996), and perhaps more extensive grazing in response to thinning soils and declining fertility. Environmental data extracted from the excavations on Pella's main mound reveal a perceptible shift from naturally occurring wild wood species to cultivated varieties, specifically willow, poplar and pine, while the lack of accessible forest species in the Umayyad period saw a greater reliance on shrubby plants, specifically oleander and tamarisk (Willcox 1992: 256). Pollen studies from lake cores taken in the Jordan Rift system have produced similar information that documents the exhaustion of the superior (in timber terms) deciduous oak species after the mid-first millennium but, later, the regeneration of inferior deciduous oak and pistachio after a short period of pine reclamation of formerly open farmlands, all the result of human activity (Baruch 1990), a conclusion backed up by recent work around Hisban. These results also match the proposed economic shift from dry-farmed valley slopes to an irrigated valley floor in early Islamic times, as argued earlier. Just as land degradation in late antique/early Islamic times might have been multi-causal, climatic and human (Bintliff 2002), so to the shift to a new agricultural regime in the eighth century resulted from various factors, both push (land impoverishment in the highlands) and pull (new valley irrigation projects).

6

Prospects: ongoing debates in Islamic archaeology

Islamic archaeology, perhaps more than other archaeologies, has little need to explain its relevance to the modern world. As the last words of this book are written in Amman during the summer of 2006, the Middle East is in the throes of another crippling crisis as increasingly vicious blows are traded across the Israel-Lebanese boarder. To many, looking in from the outside, it may seem that the region has always been in conflict and that this seemingly irresolvable state has something to do with the arrival of Islam, a view sometimes inadvertently conveyed by scholarship through dry historical accounts with an emphasis on military and dynastic events dominated by conquest, revolt, invasion and execution. The archaeology of Islamic-period Syria-Palestine has, in the last few decades, presented a very different perspective, in which arguments for social continuity, economic innovation and urban development have been presented. By drawing on new data, a more precise account is possible of how society as a whole unfolded and functioned following the expansion of Islam into Syria-Palestine in the early seventh century. The impression gained from this new analysis is in stark contrast to old views dominated by debilitating destruction and abrupt social dislocation throughout much of the region in early Islamic times, as this book has attempted to show.

The contrast between this new work and the unconsidered views that prevailed before it is as great as the cultural divide that separated Byzantium and the European west in the century leading up to the rise of Islam. As Peter Brown has observed, early in the sixth century a profound 'parting of the ways' had occurred between an authoritarian western Christendom and a more all-inclusive eastern one. The extent of this division was exposed in the unwanted counsel proffered by a visiting delegation from Rome to the emperor Anastasius, and his considered response.

> The Roman legates told Anastasius that he should impose the Catholic faith on his provincials with the firmness of a crusader. To the east Roman emperor, such advice came from another, more barbarous world. Anastasius wrote back: he would not make the streets of his cities run blood so as to impose the views of one faction on all the rest. His business was not to outlaw half his empire; it was to find a formula by which the rich spectrum of the beliefs of his subjects could be blended (Brown 1971: 148).

Early Islam likewise espoused the proven tenets of social and religious moderation championed by Anastasius, not the opposing opinions of a 'dark age' western absolutism. The lesson of encompassing, not excluding, disparate social groups was learnt well in the east, and long remembered. Much of the enormous success of the spread and, more crucially, consolidation of early Islam had to do with its flexible and eclectic outlook (Shboul 1996; Shboul and Walmsley 1998).

Released from its own restrictive intellectual constraints, archaeology in the last thirty years has endeavoured to document in fuller detail and with greater clarity the social influence of this 'world view' as seen in early Islamic Syria-Palestine, based upon a comprehensive reassessment of the material culture record. Crucial to these advances during the 1980s was the keen embrace of fresh approaches, a rigorous and ongoing questioning of existing explanations, and the creative formulation of new ideas. These research goals, the results of which have been presented and discussed in the chapters above, are certainly not exhausted and still have a long way to go. Nevertheless, the need to continue work in established areas of research should not operate as a barrier to identifying and exploring as yet poorly developed subject areas in Islamic archaeology, nor the formulation of new and as yet undefined fields. In this final chapter some of these issues are raised in a preliminary and somewhat tentative way, which perhaps reveals most about my own current interests; certainly, no claim is made that all the potential questions facing the expanding field of Islamic archaeology in Syria-Palestine are covered in what follows.

The archaeology of late antique Arab society

Scholarly perceptions and historical presentations on the arrival of Islam and on the dynastic periods that followed have created an academic fracture point in which classical antiquity has been stood in stark contrast with the Muslim medieval world. The consequences of this enforced divide in the archaeology of Syria-Palestine, repudiated but still not vanquished to this day, were outlined in Chapter 1. A significant cause of this artificially created and over-emphasised dichotomy has been a prolonged neglect of the archaeology of pre-Islamic Arab society in late antiquity, perhaps the most important cultural bridge between antiquity and Islam. Relatively greater interest has been devoted to the history and archaeology of Arab sites in the Roman period, famously Palmyra and Petra, although recent discoveries have shown that both possess a significant late antique presence. This preoccupation with the Roman period can be explained as originating in the imposing monumental aspect of these sites and the more familiar Hellenistic features they display. By way of contrast, an archaeology focusing on Arab social institutions in the fifth and sixth centuries is woefully under-represented, and yet it was precisely these communities and their age that most directly contributed to the formation of early Islamic society, not an archaic and almost forgotten Arab past.

In the last three decades, Arab history and art in the two centuries before Islam has been the subject of critical re-evaluation, in which attention has turned to assessing the source material independently and on its own grounds (e.g. Gaube 1981 on architectural decoration; Foss 1997: 245-58 on Ghassanid-Umayyad settlement continuities; compare from a written source perspective: Shahîd 1995; and, accessing topographical information, Shahîd 2002). While no consensus has yet emerged, one outcome has been an increasing recognition of the major contribution made by the many strands of late antique Arab society to a diverse and culturally encompassing early Islamic society. Unfortunately, archaeology has hardly kept up with these developments, which has further emphasised the constructed intellectual divide between antiquity and the middle ages, and given current geopolitical conditions in the region there are fewer and fewer places where archaeologists can explore these crucial questions. Nonetheless, some recent work has demonstrated the diversity and versatility of pre-Islamic Arab culture that presaged structures in the Islamic period.

Foremost has been the thorough and ongoing study of pre-Islamic Arab tribes of Syria-Palestine, especially the Ghassanids, by Irfan Shahîd, in which many longstanding preconceptions such as their nomadic lifestyle have been challenged. Working from literary sources, Shahîd (2002) documents many significant Ghassanid sites and the buildings reported as erected at each, including churches, monasteries and secular structures such as palaces, fortresses and water installations. The Ghassanid capital at Jabiyah in the Jawlan, the subject of almost no archaeological exploration, had a church, monastery, military camp and perhaps a palace, and was still sufficiently pivotal in the early seventh century to function as the first Muslim capital of Syria-Palestine for several decades (Shahîd 2002: 96-105). A major Ghassanid presence is also recorded for other sites, notably the pilgrimage centre of Rusafah, home to the cult of St Sergius and the site of a Ghassanid audience hall (Shahîd 2002: 115-33). Although Shahîd's interpretations may be disputed, his work has led the way in showing that both conceptually and in practice many elements of the Ghassanid experience in Syria-Palestine were assumed by the early Muslims, either directly and developmentally or independently by way of a shared cultural tradition.

With growing clarity, recent historical and archaeological studies are showing that pre-Islamic Arab society in the geographical unity of the Arabian Peninsula and the Syro-Jordanian steppe (Fig. 1, the *badiayh*) was advanced, structured and self-assured. Eclecticism is noticeably apparent in the fifth and sixth centuries, and this willingness to experiment was carried through with eagerness into the Umayyad period. As a result, early Islam could draw upon an extensive and common cultural experience prevalent in late antique Syria-Palestine that both appealed to the old and allowed the new. Accordingly, a future archaeology that focuses on the social and economic character of Arab communities, Christian and pagan, in the two centuries before Islam should make a major contribution to understanding the early growth, spread and consolidation of Islam, issues that still preoccupy western scholarship.

Qur'anic archaeology

Little attention has been paid to the archaeology of the Qur'an, perhaps because as a book of spiritual instruction and moral teaching it does not, on first appearance, lend itself to archaeological analysis. Furthermore, at a time when religious-based disciplines such as Biblical archaeology are coming under intense scrutiny and increasing criticism, this may not be the best time to speculate on the formulation of an archaeology that focuses on the Qur'an. Yet the task is not as impossible as it sounds, and can be enlightening.

The objective at this stage is quite straightforward and rather modest: to look at one example of Qur'anic verse and an associated site, and assess the possible contribution of archaeology to understanding the verse's context. The intention is to evaluate and cross-reference Surah (Chapter) 18 entitled 'The Cave' with the site identified as Al-Kahf al-Raqim, located southeast of Amman and traditionally linked with the cave of the Qur'an. The tale of the cave occupies only part of Surah 18 (verses 9-26; overview in Paret 1960 and a fuller analysis in Roberts 1993). Facing a challenge to their faith in a single God, the youths – the exact number of whom is not stated but may have been three, five or seven – withdrew to a cave with their dog and there took refuge for 309 years. Sleeping, the youths turned occasionally while their dog, also asleep yet alert, guarded the doorway to the cave. Upon waking, the youths guessed that they had been asleep little more than one day, not 309 years. It is a miracle story, promising resurrection, extolling the virtues of monotheism and rejecting compromise – precisely the challenges that faced the fledgling Muslim community in Makkah at the time this chapter was revealed to Prophet Muhammad.

Although the Christian legend of the sleepers locates the cave near Ephesus in Turkey, the site near Amman has a long history as being that mentioned in the Qur'an, notably in the writings of the tenth-century geographical authors al-Istakhri and al-Maqdisi, and in a later encyclopaedic work of al-Yaqut in the thirteenth century. The site has three essential elements: the cave, a small mosque above the cave, and a lower mosque positioned in front of the cave. The cave is an artificial cavity cut out of rock in the late Roman or Byzantine period and originally intended as a tomb. Facing southwards, the tomb façade is decorated and pierced by a doorway, from which steps lead down into a decorated chamber flanked with three deep arcosolia, the two lateral arcosolia having three graves apiece. Why or exactly when this particular cave can to be associated with the story in the Qur'an is not clear, but the attribution seems early.

Located above the cave is an almost square mosque with a courtyard and minaret to the east. The walls of this structure survive to a height of around 1.5 metres, and the presence of a deep mihrab in the south wall confirms that this building functioned as a mosque. Internally, two rows of columns set in line with wall pilasters suggest that the roof was supported by lateral arches. A doorway in the east wall opened out onto a portico and courtyard. On the north side the remains of a tower (minaret?) and four steps of a staircase are to be seen. While the date of this mosque is uncertain, the almost square plan, side entrance and deep mihrab matches the small mosque style seen at Umm al-Walid, Khan al-Zabib and Jabal Usays, attributable to the Umayyad period by association with larger adjacent complexes (Bujard et al. 2001: esp. 192-3).

Supporting an early attribution is the account in the Qur'an concerning the construction of a place of worship over the Cave (Qur'an 18: 22):

> ... 'Build over them
> a building; their Lord knows of them very well.'
> Said those who prevailed over their affair,
> 'We will raise over them a place of
> worship [*masjid*]'.

In other words, the account in the Qur'an makes clear reference to the construction of a building intended for worship above the cave. Surmising a historical basis to the location of the Qur'anic story, which given the cave's position near the road from Makkah to Damascus is not impossible, the current mosque cannot be that building, obviously, but the re-use of large cut stone blocks in the mosque's outer walls suggest that it may have replaced an earlier structure, perhaps originally a funerary temple later converted into a monotheistic place of worship, this being the place alluded to in the Qur'an.

The lower mosque, rectangular in shape with a long east-west axis, is located immediately in front of the cave entrance. Stylistically this mosque conforms to a well-known Mamluk type in Jordan and is, in all probability, thirteenth or fourteenth century in date, but again may represent the conversion of an earlier building.

Archaeology and the Qur'an should not be seen as incompatible fields of study, as the above may demonstrate. With due caution and realistic objectives (e.g. for 'illumination' rather than 'proof'), archaeology can increase understanding of the places and, perhaps, people mentioned in the Qur'an, just as the Qur'anic account can in some instances elucidate archaeological discoveries. Whether Qur'anic archaeology should grow into an independent field of study is questionable, but there is no good reason to discourage research into the field within the context of Islamic archaeology.

'Gap' archaeology in the post-Umayyad period

One of the still unresolved issues in the archaeology of early Islamic Syria-Palestine, and perhaps one of its most pressing, is the need to find new ways to examine the extent and nature of occupation in the region, especially the south, after the overthrow of the Umayyad dynasty in the mid-eighth century.

This question has already been raised earlier and recent evidence for settlement continuation in the later eighth and ninth centuries discussed. At this point, however, the intention is to suggest a new approach that may help in better recovering, evaluating and understanding the archaeological evidence for these centuries.

As already noted in Chapter 1, the archaeology of early Islamic Syria-Palestine has been conventionally dominated by the study of architectural monuments. When it came to evaluating social and economic conditions after the overthrow of the Umayyads, scholars have been misled into looking for more of this type of evidence by seeking concrete, monumental evidence for activity that characterised the Umayyad period in accordance with European intellectual expectations. When that evidence was not, or rarely, found the whole period was dismissed as irrelevant, and the only way to counteract such an erroneous conclusion was to nominate an appropriately ambiguous monument such as the versatile Mshatta façade, which means so many different things to different people, and, by association, the gateway on Amman citadel (above, Chapter 4). However, not many scholars have seriously entertained an Abbasid attribution for either monument.

Herein lies the fault: interpreting settlement history solely from monuments-based archaeology. Rather, the need is to adopt new strategies that adequately and accurately identify evidence of continuing cultural and economic activity without the necessity of monuments, and to apply appropriate models that explain, and do not simply dismiss, the evidence so recovered. As ceramic typo-chronologies and other dating tools improve for the long 'gap' period after the fall of the Umayyads, the major obstacle today to a more useful understanding of the archaeological data is one of perception, in which the nature of site occupation is evaluated free of stereotypical judgements such as 'squatter'.

Looking beyond the *longue durée*: resilience theory

Explicitly or implicitly, the archaeology of early Islamic Syria-Palestine has taken as one of its central theoretical doctrines the concept of the *longue durée* (explicitly, Johns 1994). This approach has served the field well until now, but are there other, more explanatory, theoretical models that may assist in understanding the raw archaeological data? Most promising for Islamic archaeology, it would seem, is resilience theory (Redman 2005; Redman and Kinzig 2003). This approach, widely applied in the social sciences, emphasises the ability of an individual, family, community or state to resist and recover from potentially destructive challenges through the construction of successful adaptive strategies, which have the effect of transforming and re-equipping existing social structures to deal with new realities. Resilience theory, therefore, emphasises the positive aspects of change in the transformation of society over time and space, especially – but not always – in times of stress when social collapse may be expected. The advantage of resilience theory is not only that it explains change, but also that it allows for multiple facets of change to happen simultaneously at different social levels, and views change as episodic and variable, at times slow and cumulative, at other times rapid to revolutionary. An important aspect of resilience theory is that change is to be expected and is inevitable, even desirable to avert social collapse. While commonly used to explain geocultural change, resilience theory is applicable to a much wider spectrum of adaptive social questions.

Resilience theory has many attractions to explain change in the archaeology of early Islamic Syria-Palestine. As a theory, it does not down-play the gravity or importance of historical events such as the Sasanid occupation, Byzantine opposition to expanding Islam, the first *fitnah* ('civil war') in the 650s, a

146

second in the 680s that culminated in the triumph of the Marwanids, or the eventual overthrow of the Umayyads, but helps to explain the mechanisms by which society at that time dealt with and overcame such serious and potentially catastrophic challenges. Likewise the social implications of natural catastrophes, such as the devastating earthquake of 749, environmental change, land degradation or plague, are also accommodated. Resilience theory still takes a long-term view, as Redman and Kinzig (2003) make clear, but allows for short bursts of sudden change and even periods of social collapse within a framework of longer-term continuity. Change and continuity are, accordingly, not opposites, but interrelated and can function in parallel. Hence, resilience theory offers an explanatory theoretical framework with which to analyse episodic occurrences of rapid social change, such as that which occurred around two generations after the Islamic expansion and that after the overthrow of the Umayyads, within the context of broader continuity in early Islamic times. It may also hold insights into the eventual urban failure of places such as Jarash, Amman and Anjar, which present as economically overspecialised and socially conservative, thereby lacking flexibility in a time of longer-term social change. The advantage of resilience theory for Islamic archaeology is that it does not ignore important historical events, but avoids the undue historical determinism that has weighed down early Islamic studies.

These are only introductory observations on the potential contribution of resilience theory to the archaeology of early Islamic Syria-Palestine, but the prospects would seem enormous, especially in dealing with issues of natural-human landscape interfaces that are increasingly relevant today. A major advantage of resilience theory is its cross-disciplinary approach and its capacity to reinvigorate archaeology by giving it contemporary relevance in a challenged and changing world.

A concluding note

This closing chapter has dealt with various new concepts and methods that may assist in the ongoing formulation of Islamic archaeology in Syria-Palestine. These issues serve as a very appropriate point at which to end this book, for the origins some twenty to thirty years ago of a well defined, problem-based Islamic archaeology for Syria-Palestine grew out of the questioning of accepted ideas and the construction of new and appropriate research models. The undoubtedly important information that emanated from these new approaches has formed the basis of this book, and from that material fresh and objective insights have been gained into the diverse and experimental nature of early Islamic society in Syria-Palestine. The establishment of Islamic archaeology on a sound intellectual base has also empowered it with contemporary relevance. As the world seeks to understand the seemingly intractable problems of the Middle East – social, political and especially environmental – Islamic archaeology has the potential of becoming a key contributor in the increasingly anxious search for sustainable solutions.

Brief chronology of early Islamic Arabia and Syria-Palestine

The Prophet Muhammad was a child of Mecca (Makkah) in the Hijaz, today part of Saudi Arabia. His exact date of birth is unknown, but was close to 570 CE. He was born into a tribal society, belonging to the Hisham clan of the Quraysh tribe. There is little doubt he existed, unlike the uncertainty that surrounds many religious figures before him. Belonging to a family of modest traders, he was orphaned when young but his situation improved following marriage to a wealthy widow Khadija (d. 619), also involved in trade. The marriage appears to have been a happy one, and among their children a daughter, Fatima, was especially favoured. In around 610 Muhammad began withdrawing from Meccan society and, according to tradition, began to receive revelations from God that were later compiled into the Qur'an (Koran). As, according to tradition, Muhammad was illiterate, these were recited – not written – revelations. The relevance of his message and his sincerity began to draw followers whose willing 'submission' (*islam*) to God (*Allah*) soon led to a conflict with the established elite of Mecca. Under pressure and as a safeguard, Muhammad relocated with a small group of the faithful to Yathrib (today Madinah) northeast of Mecca following an invitation to become a mediator to resolve the social conflicts there. His success in that task drew many more followers to his message, eventually leading to the virtual unification of the Arabian Peninsula, mostly by negotiation, into one politico-religious entity at the time of his death (632). Less successful was the attempted expansion into northern Arabia (629), invoking a military response mostly involving local Arab allies of the Byzantines which resulted in the tragic death of three leaders, including Muhammad's adopted son Zayd.

Following the death of Muhammad, the community of followers appointed one of their own, an early Companion of the Prophet by the name of Abu Bakr, as his temporal successor with the title of caliph (*khalifah,* 'successor'). After a short period of adjustment, sometimes involving armed conflict (the *Riddah* wars), the message of Islam began to spread rapidly among the tribes of northern Arabia (Syria-Palestine, Arabic *Bilad al-Sham*). This soon led to a military response, involving the Byzantines (who had in 628 dramatically and almost unexpectedly recovered the region from Sasanid-Persian occupation) and their allies, many of the latter being also Arabs. Perhaps more a civil conflict that an actual enforced conquest, Islam spread quickly in Syria-Palestine (632-40), but ultimately Islam's success was a victory of ideas, rather than one obtained by brute force alone.

Conflict over succession to the caliphate led to the great *fitnah* ('strife' or civil war that challenges the unity of the faith), in which rival claimants competed for legitimacy of succession. Mu'awiyah, governor of Syria from the Umayya clan of Mecca, was the eventual winner, but at great and permanent cost to the unity of Islam (herein lies the origin of the Sunni/Shia schism). Mu'awiyah's success resulted in the foundation of the Umayyad Dynasty (661-750), with Damascus as its capital. Mu'awiyah established many of the essential foundations of caliphal rule as a dynastic institution, although details are little known. Following another dispute over succession (the second *fitnah*, 684-92), a new line of the Umayyad family, the Marwanids, gained the caliphate unopposed and heralded in an age of brilliance in art and culture, yet one that represents a transitional age between antiquity and the Islamic middle ages and, at first, heavily derived from Byzantine and Coptic traditions. The Marwanids also paid attention to the development of governmental institutions, such as a unified administration, but it was an administration that relied almost totally on the human and financial resources of Syria-Palestine. The dynasty reached its apogee under the caliph Hisham (724-43), in whose long reign the orientation of the Islamic world began an inexorable shift to the east, this being seen in the emergence of Persian influences in the art and architecture of the period. His reign also had practical benefits, including improvements in urban conditions and economic expansion.

After Hisham's death at Rusafah in north Syria, the rapid succession of caliphs weakened focus and a revolt led by a rival Meccan family, the Abbasids, resulted in the bloody overthrow of the Umayyads. The Abbasid dynasty (temporal and spiritual power: 750-*c*. 940) was based outside of Syria-Palestine in Iraq, a geopolitical trend already evident at the end of the Umayyad period. In time a new capital was established on the Tigris River with the name of Madinat al-Salam ('city of peace'), today Baghdad. No longer the centre of events, Syria-Palestine may have languished but did not collapse, neither socially or economically. While there was little new monumental architecture commissioned by rulers or notables, especially in the south, there is plenty of archaeological and written evidence for socio-economic continuity. Indeed, by the ninth century the material culture shows a greater integration of Syria-Palestine into the wider Muslim world, in which great cities flourished (in Syria at Raqqah, on the Euphrates River) and production and trade came to predominate. In this period the social and cultural orientation of southern Syria-Palestine underwent a decisive change, in which the religious significance of its many holy places came to the fore, including Jerusalem, site of al-Aqsa ('the farthermost') mosque mentioned in the Qur'an, and al-

Mazar, site of the tombs of Zayd and the other early martyrs of 629. Many tombs of the Companions of the Prophet also were (and still are) to be found there, as were sites associated with places mentioned in the Qur'an such as the Cave of the Sleepers outside Amman. In this way, new but different life was breathed into the former Umayyad homeland.

Archaeological periods (based on D. Whitcomb)
Early Islamic 1: 600-800
Early Islamic 2: 800-1000
Middle Islamic 1: 1000-1200
Middle Islamic 2: 1200-1400

The Orthodox caliphs
Abu Bakr: 632-4
Umar b. al-Khattab: 634-44
Uthman b. Affan: 644-56
Ali b. Abu Talib: 656-61

The Umayyad caliphs
Mu'awiyah (I) b. Abu Sufyan: 661-80
Yazid (I) b. Mu'awiyah: 680-3
Mu'awiyah (II) b. Yazid: 683-4
Marwan I b. al-Hakam: 684-5
Abd al-Malik b. Marwan: 685-705
al-Walid (I) b. Abd al-Malik: 705-15
Sulayman b. Abd al-Malik: 715-17
Umar b. Abd al-Aziz: 717-20
Yazid (II) b. Abd al-Malik: 720-4
Hisham b. Abd al-Malik: 724-43
al-Walid (II) b. Yazid (II): 743-4
Yazid (III) b. al-Walid: 744
Ibrahim b. al-Walid: 744
Marwan (II) b. Muhammad: 744-50

The Abbasids (holding temporal and spiritual power)

Abu'l Abbas al-Saffah: 750-4
Al-Mansur: 754-75
Al-Mahdi: 775-85
Al-Hadi: 785-6
Harun al-Rashid: 786-809
Al-Amin: 809-13
Al-Ma'mun: 813-33
Al-Mu'tasim: 833-42
Al-Wathiq: 842-7
Al-Mutawakkil: 847-61
Al-Muntasir: 861-862
Al-Musta'in: 862-6
Al-Mu'tazz: 866-9
Al-Muhtadi: 869-70
Al-Mu'tamid: 870-92
Al-Mu'tadid: 892-902
Al-Muktafi: 902-8
Al-Muqtadir: 908-32
Al-Qahir: 932-4
Al-Radi: 934-40

Glossary

Ajnad: see *Jund*

Amsar: see *Misr*

Badiyah: The predominantly pastoral steppe-lands between the fertile areas of Mediterranean Syria-Palestine and the eastern Syro-Jordanian desert, which served as a cultural and economic corridor with the Arabian Peninsula.

Bayt/buyut: 'House', specifically referring to courtyard apartments in early Islamic times.

Dar al-imarah: The governor's palace, usually located next to the Friday mosque on the *qiblah* side.

Dinar: Early Islamic monetary unit in gold, originating in the Byzantine solidus with the name coming from Latin *denarius* (a silver denomination).

Dirham: Early Islamic monetary unit in silver, based on the Sasanid silver *drachm*.

Fals/fulus: Early Islamic monetary unit in copper used as small change, based on the Byzantine *follis*.

Fitnah: 'Strife', sedition or civil war that challenges the unity of the faith.

Hadir: A 'camp', also 'settlement', a suburb of a major urban centre occupied by Arab tribes in the pre-Islamic period, at first transient but later permanent; 'an ethnic suburb with permanent architecture, the locus of tribal sedentarisation' (Whitcomb 2000a: 10). Examples include Hadir Qinnasrin and Hadir Aleppo. From them sprung, conceptually and sometimes physically, the *misr/amsar*.

Hirah: Military encampment of the Pre-Islamic Arabs.

Jazirah: Literally 'island', referring geographically to an area of land between the Euphrates and Tigris rivers, today in northeast Syria and northern Iraq.

Jund/ajnad: A '(military) province', the administrative divisions of Syria-Palestine in early Islamic times (see Fig. 7). Each *jund* was further subdivided into a number of *kurah* (districts), often urban-based.

Madinah/mudun: A 'city', more used as a technical term than a description of size or importance. In the early Islamic period, a *madinah* had five essential elements: a mosque, a palace, markets, a bath and water utilities.

Masjid: A place of worship (literally: a place of prostration); a mosque (which entered European languages via the Spanish *mezquita*).

Mihrab: Half-circular recess in the *qiblah* wall of a mosque, serving as a focal point for prayer.

Misr/amsar: An 'encampment', primarily in reference to new, formal settlements founded next to the existing towns of Syria-Palestine. Usually they were walled and orthogonally planned, with straight streets, a centrally-placed mosque, a *dar al-imarah* and serving administrative functions. Examples include Aylah and al-Ramlah (Whitcomb 1995a).

Qasr/qusur/qusayr: A 'castle', used in reference to the many rural princely establishments founded in Syria-Palestine by the Umayyads. They varied enormously in size and function, but focused on one or more elite buildings often richly decorated. Examples include Qasr al-Hayr al-Sharqi (Grabar et al. 1978), Khirbat al-Mafjar ('Hisham's Palace', Hamilton 1959) and Qusayr Amra (*qusayr* being the diminutive of *qasr*).

Qiblah: Direction of prayer, always towards Mecca, site of the Holy Sanctuary with the Ka'bah, located in the Hijaz of the Arabian Peninsula.

Shahadah: The Muslim proclamation of Faith: 'There is no god but God (Allah) alone; Muhammad is the Messenger of God.'

Suq: Urban market place.

For further details, consult entries in *The Encyclopaedia of Islam,* second edition (Leiden, Brill).

Bibliography

Aharoni, Y., 1964. *Excavations at Ramat Rahel, Seasons 1961 and 1962* (Rome: Università degli studi Centro di studi semitici).

Album, S. and Goodwin, T., 2002. *Sylloge of Islamic Coins in the Ashmolean* vol. 1 *The Pre-reform Coinage of the Early Islamic Period* (Oxford: Ashmolean Museum).

Allan, J.W., 1991. New additions to the new edition. *Muqarnas* 8: 12-22.

Almagro, A. and Arce, I., 2001. The Umayyad town planning of the citadel of 'Amman. *Studies in the History and Archaeology of Jordan* vol. 7 (Amman: Department of Antiquities of Jordan), 659-65.

'Amr, K. and Schick, R., 2001. The pottery from Humeima: the closed corpus from the Lower Church. In E. Villeneuve and P.M. Watson (eds), *La céramique byzantine et proto-islamique en Syrie-Jordanie (IVe-VIIIe siècles apr. J.-C.)* (Beyrouth: IFAPO), 107-27.

As'ad, K. and Stepniowski, F.M., 1989. The Umayyad suq in Palmyra. *Damaszener Mitteilungen* 4: 205-23.

Avner, U. and Magness, J., 1998. Early Islamic settlement in the southern Negev. *Bulletin of the American Schools of Oriental Research* 310: 39-57.

Avni, G., 1994. Early mosques in the Negev Highlands: new archaeological evidence on Islamic penetration of southern Palestine. *Bulletin of the American Schools of Oriental Research* 294: 83-99.

Avni, G., 1996. *Nomads, Farmers, and Town-Dwellers: Pastoralist-Sedentist Interaction in the Negev Highlands, Sixth-Eighth Centuries CE* (Jerusalem: Israel Antiquities Authority).

Bacharach, J.L., 1996. Marwanid Umayyad building activities: speculations on patronage. *Muqarnas* 13: 27-44.

Balty, J., 1984. *Apamée de Syrie: bilan des recherches archéologiques, 1973-1979. Aspects de l'architecture domestique d'Apamée: actes du colloque tenu à Bruxelles les 29, 30 et 31 mai 1980* (Bruxelles: Centre belge de recherches archéologiques à Apamée de Syrie).

Bartl, K., 1994. *Frühislamische Besiedlung im Balîḫ-Tal/Nordsyrien* (Berlin: Dietrich Reimer Verlag).

Bartl, K., 1996. Balîḫ Valley Survey: settlements of the late Roman/early Byzantine and Islamic period. In K. Bartl and S.R. Hauser (eds), *Continuity and Change in Northern Mesopotamia from the Hellenistic to the Early Islamic Period* (Berlin: Dietrich Reimer), 333-48.

Baruch, U., 1990. Palynological evidence of human impact on the vegetation as recorded in Late Holocene lake sediments in Israel. In S. Bottema, G. Entjes-Nieborg, and W. van Zeist (eds), *Man's Role in the Shaping of the Eastern Mediterranean Landscape* (Rotterdam: Balkema), 283-93.

Bates, M.L., 1976. The Arab-Byzantine bronze coinage of Syria: an innovation

Bibliography

by 'Abd al-Malik. *A Colloquium in Memory of George Carpenter Miles (1904-1975)* (New York: American Numismatic Society), 16-27.

Bates, M.L., 1986. History, geography and numismatics in the first century of Islamic coinage. *Revue suisse de numismatique* 65: 231-62.

Bell, G.L., 1907. *The Desert and the Sown* (London: Heinemann).

Ben-Dov, M., 1985. *In the Shadow of the Temple: The Discovery of Ancient Jerusalem* (Jerusalem: Keter).

Bijovsky, G., 2002. A hoard of Byzantine solidi from Bet She'an in the Umayyad period. *Revue numismatique* 158: 161-227.

Bintliff, J., 2002. Time, process and catastrophism in the study of Mediterranean alluvial history: a review. *World Archeology* 33: 417-35.

Bisheh, G., 1987. Qasr al-Mshatta in the light of a recently found inscription. In A. Hadidi (ed.), *Studies in the History and Archaeology of Jordan* vol. 3 (Amman: Department of Antiquities of Jordan), 193-7.

Bisheh, G. and Humbert, J.-B., 1997. Le surprenant brasero omeyyade trouvé à Mafraq. In E. Delpont (ed.), *Jordanie: sur les pas des archéologues* (Paris: Institut du Monde Arabe), 157-75.

Bowersock, G.W., 1990. *Hellenism in Late Antiquity* (Ann Arbor: University of Michigan Press).

Bowersock, G.W., 2006. *Mosaics as History: The Near East from Late Antiquity to Islam* (Cambridge, Mass.: Harvard University Press).

Brown, P., 1971. *The World of Late Antiquity, From Marcus Aurelius to Muhammad* (London: Thames & Hudson).

Brown, R.M., 1991. Ceramics from the Kerak Plateau. In J.M. Miller (ed.), *Archaeological Survey of the Kerak Plateau* (Atlanta, Ga.: Scholars Press), 168-279.

Brünnow, R.-E. and Domaszewski, A. von, 1904-1909. *Die provincia Arabia auf Grund zweier in den Jahren 1897 und 1898 unternommenen Reisen und der Berichte früherer Reisender,* 3 vols (Strassburg: K.J. Trübner).

Bujard, J., Genequand, D., and Trillen, W., 2001. Umm al-Walid et Khan az-Zabib, deux établissements omeyyades en limite du désert Jordanien. In B. Geyer (ed.), *Conquête de la steppe: et appropriation des terres sur les marges arides du Croissant fertile* (Lyon: Maison de l'Orient Méditerranéen-Jean Pouilloux), 189-218.

Butler, H.C., 1907-49. *Syria: Publications of the Princeton University Archaeological Expeditions to Syria in 1904-5 and 1909* (Leiden).

Butzer, K.W., 2005. Environmental history in the Mediterranean world: cross-disciplinary investigation of cause-and-effect for degradation and soil erosion. *Journal of Archaeological Science* 32: 1773-800.

Charles, M. and Hoppé, C., 2003. The effects of irrigation on the weeds floras of winter cereal crops in Wadi Ibn Hamad (Southern Jordan). *Levant* 35: 213-30.

Chehab, H.K., 1993. On the identification of 'Anjar ('Ayn al-Jarr) as an Umayyad Foundation. *Muqarnas* 10 (Essays in Honor of Oleg Grabar), 42-8.

Creswell, K.A.C., 1932. *Early Muslim Architecture* vol. 1 *Umayyads A.D. 622-750* (Oxford: Clarendon Press).

Creswell, K.A.C., 1940. *Early Muslim Architecture* vol. 2 *Early Abbasids, Umayyads of Cordova, Aghlabids, Tulunids and Samanids, A.D. 751-905* (Oxford: Clarendon Press).

Creswell, K.A.C., 1958. *A Short Account of Early Muslim Architecture* (Harmondsworth: Penguin).

Creswell, K.A.C., 1969. *Early Muslim Architecture* vol. 1 *Umayyads, A.D. 622-750.* 2nd edn (Oxford: Clarendon Press).

Bibliography

Creswell, K.A.C. and Allan, J.W., 1989. *A Short Account of Early Muslim Architecture* (London: Scolar Press).

Crowfoot, J.W., 1931. *Churches at Jerash* (London: British School of Archaeology in Jerusalem).

Crowfoot, J.W., 1938. The Christian churches. In C.H. Kraeling (ed.), *Gerasa, City of the Decapolis* (New Haven: American Schools of Oriental Research), 171-262.

Delogu, P., 1998. Reading Pirenne again. In R. Hodges and W. Bowden (eds), *The Sixth Century: Production, Distribution, and Demand* (Leiden: Brill), 15-40.

Di Segni, L., 1999. Epigraphic documentation on building in the provinces of *Palaestina* and *Arabia*, 4th-7th c. In J.H. Humphrey (ed.), *The Roman and Byzantine Near East* vol. 2 *Some Recent Archaeological Research* (Portsmouth, RI: Journal of Roman Archaeology), 149-78.

Di Segni, L., 2003. Christian epigraphy in the Holy Land: new discoveries. *ARAM* 15: 247-67.

Donner, F.M., 1981. *The Early Islamic Conquests* (Princeton, NJ: Princeton University Press).

Donner, H. and Cüppers, H., 1977. *Die Mosackkarte von madeba* (Wiesbaden: Harrassowitz).

Dothan, M. and Johnson, B.L., 2000. *Hammath Tiberias* vol. 2 *Late Synagogues* (Jerusalem: Israel Exploration Society).

Dunlop, D.M., 1971. *Arab Civilisation to A.D. 1500* (London: Longman).

Dussart, O., 1998. *Le verre en Jordanie et en Syrie du Sud* (Beyrouth: Institut français d'archéologie du Proche-Orient).

Eastwood, G.M., 1992. The Pella textiles. In A.W. McNicoll, J. Hanbury-Tenison, J.B. Hennessy, T.F. Potts, R.H. Smith, A. Walmsley, and P. Watson (eds), *Pella in Jordan 2. The Second Interim Report of the Joint University of Sydney and College of Wooster Excavations at Pella 1982-1985* (Sydney: Mediterranean Archaeology), 257-65.

Eddé, A.-M. and Sodini, J.-P., 2005. Les villages de Syrie du Nord au VIIe au XIIIe siècle. In J. Lefort, C. Morrisson, and J.-P. Sodini (eds), *Les villages dans l'Empire byzantin (IVe-XVe siècle)* (Paris: Lethielleux), 465-83.

Elad, A., 1992. Two identical inscriptions from the Jund Filastin from the reign of the 'Abbasid Caliph, al-Muqtadir. *Journal of the Economic and Social History of the Orient* 35: 301-60.

Enzel, Y., Bookman (Ken Tor), R., Sharon, D., Gvirtzman, H., Dayan, U., Ziv, B., and Stein, M., 2003. Late Holocene climates of the Near East deduced from Dead Sea level variations and modern regional winter rainfall. *Quaternary Research* 60: 263-73.

Ettinghausen, R., Grabar, O., and Jenkins-Madina, M., 2001. *The Art and Architecture of Islam 650-1250*, 2nd edn (New Haven: Yale University Press).

Fahd, T., 1997. Shâ'ir. *Encyclopaedia of Islam*, new edn, vol. 9 (Leiden: Brill), 225-8.

Fiema, Z.T., 2002. Late-antique Petra and its hinterland: recent research and new interpretations. In J.H. Humphrey (ed.), *The Roman and Byzantine Near East* vol. 3 (Portsmouth, RI: Journal of Roman Archaeology, Supplementary Series no. 49), 191-252.

Fine, S., 2000. Iconoclasm and the art of the late-antique Palestinian synagogues. In L.I. Levine and Z. Weiss (eds), *From Dura to Sepphoris: Studies in Jewish Art and Society in Late Antiquity* (Portsmouth, R.I.: Journal of Roman Archaeology), 183-94.

Bibliography

Fitzgerald, G.M., 1931. *Beth-Shan Excavations 1921-23. The Arab and Byzantine Levels* (Philadelphia: University of Pennsylvania).

Foerster, G., 1992. The Ancient synagogues of the Galilee. In L.I. Levine (ed.), *The Galilee in Late Antiquity* (New York: Jewish Theological Seminary of America), 289-319.

Foote, R., 1999. Umayyad markets and manufacturing: evidence for a commercialized and industrializing economy in early Islamic Bilad al-Sham. Unpublished PhD thesis, Harvard University.

Foote, R., 2000. Commerce, industrial expansion and orthogonal planning: mutually compatible terms in settlements of Bilâd al-Shâm during the Umayyad period. *Mediterranean Archaeology* 13: 25-38.

Foote, R. and Oleson, J.P., 1996. Humeima Excavation Project, 1995-96. *Fondation Max Van Berchem Bulletin* 10: 1-4.

Foss, C., 1995. The Near Eastern countryside in late antiquity: a review article. In J.H. Humphrey (ed.), *The Roman and Byzantine Near East: Some Recent Archaeological Research* (Ann Arbor: Journal of Roman Archaeology, Supplementary Series no. 14), 213-34.

Foss, C., 1997. Syria in transition, A.D. 550-750: an archaeological approach. *Dumbarton Oaks Papers* 51: 189-269.

Foss, C., 2004. The coinage of the first century of Islam (review of Stephen Album and Tony Goodwin, *Sylloge of Islamic Coins in the Ashmolean Museum* vol. 1 *The Pre-Reform Coinage of the Early Islamic Period* (Ashmolean Museum, Oxford 2002)). *Journal of Roman Archaeology* 17.2: 748-60.

Fowden, G., 2004. *Qusayr 'Amra: Art and the Umayyad Elite in Late Antique Syria* (Berkeley: University of California Press).

Frankel, R., Getzov, N., Aviam, M., and Degani, A., 2001. *Settlement Dynamics and Regional Diversity in Ancient Upper Galilee: Archaeological Survey of Upper Galilee* (Jerusalem: Israel Antiquities Authority).

Franken, H.J. and Kalsbeek, J., 1975. *Potters of a Medieval Village in the Jordan Valley* (Amsterdam: North Holland).

Freestone, I.C., Gorin-Rosen, Y., and Hughes, M.J., 2000. Primary glass from Israel and the production of glass in late antiquity and the early Islamic period. In M.-D. Nenna (ed.), *La route du verre: ateliers primaires et secondaires du second millénaire av. J.-C. au moyen âge* (Lyon: Maison de l'Orient Méditerranéen-Jean Pouilloux), 65-83.

Gatier, P.-L., 1987. Une lettre du pape Grégoire le Grand à Marianus évêque de Gerasa. *Syria* 64: 131-5.

Gatier, P.-L., 2005. Les villages du Proche-Orient protobyzantin: nouvelles perspectives (1994-2004). In J. Lefort, C. Morrisson and J.-P. Sodini (eds), *Les villages dans l'Empire byzantin (IVe-XVe siècle)* (Paris: Lethielleux), 101-19.

Gaube, H., 1981. Arabs in sixth-century Syria: some archaeological observations. *Bulletin of the British Society for Middle Eastern Studies* 8: 93-8.

Gautier, A., 1984. La faune de quelques maisons d'Apamée. In J. Balty (ed.), *Apamée de Syrie: bilan des recherches archéologiques, 1973-1979. Aspects de l'architecture domestique d'Apamée: actes du colloque tenu à Bruxelles les 29, 30 et 31 mai 1980* (Bruxelles: Centre belge de recherches archéologiques à Apamée de Syrie), 305-60.

Genequand, D., 2004a. Al-Bakhra (Avatha), from the Tetrarchic fort to the Umayyad castle. *Levant* 36: 225-42.

Genequand, D., 2004b. Rapport préliminaire de la campagne de fouille 2003 à Qasr al-Hayr al-Sharqi et al-Bakhra' (Syrie). *Schweizerisch-Liechtensteinis-*

che Stiftung für Archäologische Forschungen im Ausland. Jahresbericht 2003 (Zurich), 69-98.

Genequand, D., 2006. Umayyad castles: the shift from late antique military architecture to early Islamic palatial building. In H. Kennedy (ed.), *Muslim Military Architecture in Greater Syria. From the Coming of Islam to the Ottoman Period* (Leiden: Brill), 3-25.

Geva, H., 1993. Jerusalem: The Byzantine Period. In E. Stern (ed.), *New Encyclopaedia of Archaeological Excavations in the Holy Land* vol. 2 (Jerusalem: Israel Exploration Society), 768-81.

Gibson, S. and Vitto, F., 1999. *Ramla: The Development of a Town from the Early Islamic to Ottoman Periods* (Jerusalem: Israel Antiquities Authority).

Gichon, M., 1974. Fine Byzantine Wares from the South of Israel. *Palestine Exploration Quarterly* 106: 119-39.

Goitein, S., 1983. *A Mediterranean Society: The Jewish Communities of the Arab World as Portrayed in the Documents of the Cairo Geniza. Daily Life* (Berkeley: University of California Press).

Gonnella, J., 2006. The Citadel of Aleppo: recent studies. In H. Kennedy (ed.), *Muslim Military Architecture in Greater Syria. From the Coming of Islam to the Ottoman Period* (Leiden: Brill), 165-75.

Goodwin, T., 2005. *Arab-Byzantine Coinage* (London: Nour Foundation/Azimuth Editions).

Gorin-Rosen, Y., 2000. The ancient glass industry in Israel. Summary of finds and new discoveries. In M.-D. Nenna (ed.), *La route du verre: ateliers primaires et secondaires du second millénaire av. J.-C. au Moyen Âge* (Lyon: Maison de l'Orient Méditerranéen-Jean Pouilloux), 49-63.

Grabar, O., 1976. Islamic art and archaeology. In L. Binder (ed.), *The Study of the Middle East* (New York: Wiley), 229-63.

Grabar, O., 1987. The date and meaning of Mshatta. *Dumbarton Oaks Papers* 41: 243-7.

Grabar, O., 1993. Umayyad palaces reconsidered. *Ars Orientalis* 23: 93-108.

Grabar, O., Holod, R., Knustad, J., and Trousdale, W., 1978. *City in the Desert: Qasr al Hayr East* (Cambridge, Mass.: Harvard University Press).

Graf, D.F., 2001. Town and countryside in Roman Arabia during late antiquity. In T.S. Burns and J. Eadie (eds), *Urban Centers and Rural Contexts in Late Antiquity* (East Lansing: Michigan State University Press), 219-38.

Guérin, A., 1997. Organisation de l'espace habité en milieu rural à la période islamique. In C. Castel, M. Maqdissi, and F. Villeneuve (eds), *Les maisons dans la Syrie antique du IIIe millénaire aux débuts de l'Islam: pratique et représentations de l'espace domestique: actes du Colloque International, Damas, 27-30 juin 1992* (Beyrouth: IFAPO), 195-202.

Guidoboni, E., Comastri, A., and Traina, G., 1994. *Catalogue of Ancient Earthquakes in the Mediterranean Area up to the 10th Century* (Rome: Istituto nazionale di geofisica).

Haase, C.-P., 1995. al-Rusâfa. *Encyclopaedia of Islam*, new edn, vol. 8: 629-31.

Haase, C.-P., 1996. Madinat al-Far: the regional late antique tradition of an early Islamic foundation. In K. Bartl and S.R. Hauser (eds), *Continuity and Change in Northern Mesopotamia from the Hellenistic to the Early Islamic Period* (Berlin: Dietrich Reimer), 165-71.

Haase, C.-P., 2006. The excavations at Madinat al-Far/Husn Maslama on the Balikh road. In H. Kennedy (ed.), *Muslim Military Architecture in Greater Syria. From the Coming of Islam to the Ottoman Period* (Leiden: Brill), 54-60.

Haiman, M., 1995a. Agriculture and nomad-state relations in the Negev Desert in the Byzantine and early Islamic periods. *Bulletin of the American Schools of Oriental Research* 297: 29-53.

Haiman, M., 1995b. An early Islamic period farm at Nahal Mitnan in the Negev Highlands. *'Atiqot* 26: 1-13.

Haldon, J., 1995. Seventh-century continuities: the *Ajnad* and the 'thematic myth'. In A. Cameron (ed.), *The Byzantine and Early Islamic Near East 3. State, Resources and Armies* (Princeton, NJ: Darwin Press), 379-423.

Hamilton, R.W., 1959. *Khirbat al Mafjar: An Arabian Mansion in the Jordan Valley* (Oxford: Clarendon).

Hamilton, R.W., 1978. Khirbat al Mafjar: the Bath Hall reconsidered. *Levant* 10: 126-38.

Hamilton, R.W., 1988. *Walid and His Friends. An Umayyad Tragedy* (Oxford: Board of the Faculty of Oriental Studies/Oxford University Press).

Harding, G.L., 1959. *The Antiquities of Jordan* (London: Lutterworth Press).

Hayes, J.W., 1972. *Late Roman Pottery. A Catalogue of Roman Fine Wares* (London: British School at Rome).

Hayes, J.W., 1980. *A Supplement to Late Roman Pottery* (London: British School at Rome).

Heidemann, S., 2006. The history of the industrial and commercial area of 'Abbasid Al-Raqqa, called Al-Raqqa Al-Muhtariqa. *Bulletin of the School of Oriental and African Studies* 69: 33-52.

Heidemann, S. and Becker, A., 2003. *Raqqa II: Die Islamische Stadt* (Mainz: P. von Zabern).

Henderson, J., 1999. Archaeological and scientific evidence for the production of early Islamic glass in al-Raqqa, Syria. *Levant* 31: 225-40.

Henderson, J., McLoughlin, S.D., and McPhail, D.S., 2004. Radical changes in Islamic glass technology: evidence for conservatism and experimentation with new glass recipes from early and middle Islamic Raqqa, Syria. *Archaeometry* 46: 439-68.

Heusch, J.-C. and Meinecke, M., 1985. Grabungen im 'abbasidischen Palastareal von ar-Raqqa/ar-Rafiqa 1982-1983. *Damaszener Mitteilungen* 2: 85-105.

Hillenbrand, R., 1981. Islamic art at the crossroads: East verses West at Mshattâ. In A. Daneshvari (ed.), *Essays in Islamic Art and Architecture in Honor of Katharina Otto-Dorn* (Malibu: Undena Publications), 63-86.

Hillenbrand, R., 1999. 'Anjar and early Islamic urbanism. In G.P. Brogiolo and B. Ward-Perkins (eds), *The Idea and Ideal of the Town between Late Antiquity and the Early Middle Ages* (Leiden: E.J. Brill), 59-98.

Hirschfeld, Y., 1999. Imperial building activity during the reign of Justinian and pilgrimage to the Holy Land in light of the excavations on Mt. Berenice, Tiberias. *Revue biblique* 106: 236-49.

Hirschfeld, Y., 2003. Social aspects of the late-antique village of Shivta. *Journal of Roman Archaeology* 16: 392-408.

Hirschfeld, Y., 2004a. A climatic change in the Early Byzantine period? Some archaeological evidence. *Palestine Exploration Fund Quarterly* 136: 133-49.

Hirschfeld, Y., 2004b. *Excavations at Tiberias, 1989-1994* (Jerusalem: Israel Antiquities Authority).

Hirschfeld, Y., Gutfeld, O., Khamis, E., and Amir, R., 2000. A hoard of Fatimid bronze vessels from Tiberias. *Al-'Usur al-Wusta* 12: 1-7, 27.

Holum, K.G., 1992. Archaeological evidence for the fall of Byzantine Caesarea. *Bulletin of the American Schools of Oriental Research* 286: 73-85.

Holum, K.G. and Hohlfelder, R.L., 1988. *King Herod's Dream: Caesarea on the Sea* (New York: Norton).

Bibliography

Horwitz, L.K., 1998. Animal exploitation during the early Islamic period in the Negev: the fauna from Elat-Elot. *Atiqot* 36: 27-38.

Hoyland, R., 2006. New documentary texts and the early Islamic state. *Bulletin of the School of Oriental and African Studies* 69: 395-416.

Ibn Hawqal, trans. Kramers and Weit, 1964. *Configuration de la terre (Kitab Surat al-Ard)* (Paris/Beyrouth: Editions G.-P. Maisonneuve & Larose/Commission internationale pour la traduction des chefs d'oeuvre).

Ilan, Z., 1989. The synagogue and *Beth Midrash* of Meroth. In R. Hachlili (ed.), *Ancient Synagogues in Israel: third-seventh century C.E. Proceedings of Symposium, University of Hafia* (sic), *May 1987* (Oxford: BAR), 21-42.

Jaussen, A. and Savignac, R., 1909-22. *Mission archéologique en Arabie (mars – mai 1907)*, 3 vols (Paris: Leroux).

Johns, J., 1992. Islamic settlement in Ard al-Karak. In S. Tell, G. Bisheh, F. Zayadine, K. 'Amr, and M. Zaghloul (eds), *Studies in the History and Archaeology of Jordan* vol. 4 (Amman: Department of Antiquities of Jordan), 363-8.

Johns, J., 1994. The *longue durée*: state and settlement strategies in southern Transjordan across the Islamic centuries. In E.L. Rogan and T. Tell (eds), *Village, Steppe and State. The Social Origins of Modern Jordan* (London: British Academic Press), 1-31.

Johns, J., 1998. The rise of Middle Islamic hand-made geometrically-painted ware in Bilâd al-Shâm (11th-13th centuries A.D.). In R.-P. Gayraud (ed.), *Colloque international d'archéologie islamique: IFAO, Le Caire, 3-7 février 1993* (Cairo: Institut français d'archéologie Orientale), 65-93.

Johns, J., 1999. The 'House of the Prophet' and the concept of the mosque. In J. Johns (ed.), *Bayt al-Maqdis: Jerusalem and Early Islam* (Oxford: Oxford University Press), 59-112.

Johns, J., 2003. Archaeology and the history of early Islam: the first seventy years. *Journal of the Economic and Social History of the Orient* 46: 411-36.

Kennedy, H., 1985a. From *polis* to *madina*: urban change in late antique and early Islamic Syria. *Past & Present* 106: 3-27.

Kennedy, H., 1985b. The last century of Byzantine Syria: a reinterpretation. *Byzantinische Forschungen* 10: 141-84.

Kennedy, H., 1999. Islam. In G.W. Bowersock, P. Brown, and O. Grabar (eds), *Late Antiquity. A Guide to the Postclassical World* (Cambridge, Mass.: Belknap Press of Harvard University Press), 219-37.

Kennedy, H. and Liebeschuetz, J.H.W.G., 1989. Antioch and the Villages of Northern Syria in the Fifth and Sixth Centuries A.D.: Trends and Problems. *Nottingham Medieval Studies* 32: 65-90.

Khamis, E., 2001. Two wall mosaic inscriptions from the Umayyad market place in Bet Shean/Baysan. *Bulletin of the School of Oriental and African Studies* 64: 159-76.

Kisnawi, A., de Jesus, P., and Rihani, B., 1983. Preliminary report on the mining survey, Northwest Hijaz, 1982. *Atlal* 7: 76-83.

Knauf, E.A., 1984. Umm al-Jimal: an Arab town in late antiquity. *Revue biblique* 91: 578-86.

Knauf, E.A., 1987. Aspects of historical topography relating to the battles of Mu'ta and the Yarmuk. In M.A. Bakhit (ed.), *Proceedings of the Second Symposium on the History of Bilad al-Sham during the Early Islamic Period, up to 40 A.H. / 640 A.D.* (Amman: The University of Jordan), 73-8.

Kraeling, C.H., 1938. *Gerasa, City of the Decapolis* (New Haven: American Schools of Oriental Research).

162

Bibliography

Kraemer, C.J., 1958. *Excavations at Nessana 3. Non-Literary Papyri* (Princeton: Princeton University Press).

Lender, Y., 1990. *Archaeological Survey of Israel: Map of Har Nafha (196) 12-01* (Jerusalem: Israel Antiquities Authority.).

Lenzen, C.J. and Knauf, E.A., 1987. Beit Ras/Capitolias. A preliminary evaluation of the archaeological and textual evidence. *Syria* 64: 21-46.

Lester, A., 1999. The metal hoard of Caesarea. In A. Raban, R. Toueg, Y.D. Arnon, R. Pollak, and A. Lester (eds), *The Richness of Islamic Caesarea* (Haifa: Reuben and Edith Hecht Museum), 36*-41*.

Levine, L.I., 1982. *Ancient Synagogues Revealed* (Jerusalem: Israel Exploration Society).

Levine, L.I. and Netzer, E., 1986. *Excavations at Caesarea Maritima 1975, 1976, 1979 – Final Report* (Jerusalem: Institute of Archaeology, Hebrew University).

Liebeschuetz, W., 2000. Late late antiquity (6th and 7th centuries) in the cities of the Roman Near East. *Mediterraneo Antico* 3: 43-75.

Lucke, B., Schmidt, M., al-Saad, Z., Bens, O., and Huttl, R.F., 2005. The abandonment of the Decapolis region in Northern Jordan – forced by environmental change? *Quaternary International* 135: 65-81.

Luz, N., 1997. The construction of an Islamic city in Palestine: the case of Umayyad al-Ramla. *Journal of the Royal Asiatic Society* 37: 27-54.

MacAdam, H.I., 1986. Some notes on the Umayyad occupation of North-East Jordan. In P. Freeman and D. Kennedy (eds), *The Defence of the Roman and Byzantine East* (Oxford: BAR), 531-47.

Macaulay, R., 1953. *Pleasure of Ruins* (London: Weidenfeld and Nicolson).

Mackensen, M., 1984. *Resafa I. Eine befestigte spätantike Anlage vor den Stadtmauern von Resafa: Ausgrabungen und spätantike Kleinfunde eines Surveys im Umland von Resafa-Sergiupolis* (Mainz: P. von Zabern).

Magness, J., 1993. *Jerusalem Ceramic Chronology, circa 200-800 CE* (Sheffield: Sheffield Academic Press).

Magness, J., 1997. The chronology of Capernaum in the early Islamic period. *Journal of the American Oriental Society* 117: 481-6.

Magness, J., 2003. *The Archaeology of the Early Islamic Settlement in Palestine* (Winona Lake: Eisenbrauns).

Meinecke, M., 1991. Raqqa on the Euphrates: recent excavations at the residence of Harun er-Rashid. *The Near East in Antiquity* 2: 17-32.

Meinecke, M., 1995. al-Rakka, *Encyclopaedia of Islam*, new edn, vol. 8 (Leiden: Brill), 410-14.

Meinecke, M., 1998. From Mschatta to Samarra: the architecture of ar-Raqqa and its decoration. In R.-P. Gayraud (ed.), *Colloque international d'archéologie islamique: IFAO, Le Caire, 3-7 février 1993* (Cairo: Institut français d'archéologie Orientale), 141-8.

Melkawi, A., 'Amr, K., and Whitcomb, D.S., 1994. The excavation of two seventh century pottery kilns at Aqaba. *Annual of the Department of Antiquities of Jordan* 38: 447-68.

Merrill, S., 1881. *East of the Jordan: a Record of Travel and Observation in the Countries of Moab, Gilead, and Bashan* (London: Richard Bentley & Son).

Meyer, J.-W., 2006. Recent excavations in early Abbasid Kharab Sayyar. In H. Kennedy (ed.), *Muslim Military Architecture in Greater Syria. From the Coming of Islam to the Ottoman Period* (Leiden: Brill), 45-53.

Michel, A., 2001. *Les églises d'époque byzantine et umayyade de Jordanie (provinces d'Arabie et de Palestine), Ve-VIIIe siècle: typologie architecturale et aménagements liturgiques (avec catalogue des monuments)* (Turnhout: Brepols).

Morrisson, C., 1972. Le trésor byzantin de Nikertai. *Revue belge de numismatique et de sigillographie* 118: 29-91.

Muqaddasi (al-Maqdisi), trans. Collins, 1994. *The Best Divisions for the Knowledge of the Regions (Ahsan al-Taqasim fi ma'rifat al-Aqalim)* (Reading: Garnet).

Museum with No Frontiers, 2000. *The Umayyads. The Rise of Islamic Art* (Vienna: Arab Institute for Research and Publishing).

Musil, A., 1907a. *Arabia Petraea* (Wien).

Musil, A., 1907b. *Kusejr 'Amra* (Wien).

Negev, A., 1974. The churches of the central Negev. An archaeological survey. *Revue biblique* 81: 400-22.

Negev, A., 1997. *The Architecture of Oboda: Final Report* (Jerusalem: Institute of Archaeology, Hebrew University of Jerusalem).

Northedge, A., 1992. *Studies on Roman and Islamic 'Amman* vol. 1 *The Excavations of Mrs C-M Bennett and Other Investigations* (Oxford: British Institute at Amman for Archaeology and History/ Oxford University Press).

Northedge, A., 1999. Archaeology and Islam. In G. Barker (ed.), *Companion Encyclopedia of Archaeology* (London: Routledge), 1077-106.

Northedge, A., 2000. Entre Amman et Samarra: l'archéologie et les élites au début de l'Islam (VIIe-IXe siècle). Habilitation, Université de Paris I (Panthéon-Sorbonne), Paris.

Northedge, A., 2001. Thoughts on the introduction of polychrome glazed pottery in the Middle East. In E. Villeneuve and P.M. Watson (eds), *La céramique byzantine et proto-islamique en Syrie-Jordanie (IVe-VIIIe siècles apr. J.-C.)* (Beyrouth: Institut français d'archéologie du Proche-Orient), 207-14.

Northedge, A., 2006. *Historical Topography of Samarra* (London: British School of Archaeology in Iraq).

O'Hea, M., 2001. Some problems in early Islamic glassware, *Annales du 15e congrès de l'association internationale pour l'histoire du verre* (New York), 133-7.

Orssaud, D., 1992. Le passage de la céramique byzantine à la céramique islamique. In P. Canivet and J.-P. Rey-Coquais (eds), *La Syrie de Byzance à l'Islam VIIe-VIIIe siècles: actes du colloque international* (Damascus: Institut français de Damas), 219-28.

Ovadiah, A., 1970. *Corpus of the Byzantine Churches in the Holy Land* (Bonn: Peter Hanstein).

Ovadiah, A., 1993. Early churches. In E. Stern (ed.), *New Encyclopaedia of Archaeological Excavations in the Holy Land* vol. 1 (Jerusalem: Israel Exploration Society), 305-9.

Paret, R., 1960. Ashâb al-Kahf. *Encyclopaedia of Islam*, new edn, vol. 1 (Leiden: Brill), 691.

Parker, S.T., 2000. The defense of Palestine and Transjordan from Diocletian to Heraclius. In L.E. Stager, J.A. Greene, and M.D. Coogan (eds), *The Archaeology of Jordan and Beyond. Essays in Honor of James A. Sauer* (Winona Lake: Eisenbrauns), 367-88.

Parker, S.T., 2006. *The Roman Frontier in Central Jordan: Final Report on the Limes Arabicus Project, 1980-1989* (Washington, D.C.: Dumbarton Oaks).

Patrich, J., 1995. Church, state and the transformation of Palestine – the Byzantine period (324-640 CE). In T.E. Levy (ed.), *The Archaeology of Society in the Holy Land* (London: Leicester University Press), 470-87.

Bibliography

Pentz, P., 1992. *The Invisible Conquest. The Ontogenesis of Sixth and Seventh Century Syria* (Copenhagen: National Museum of Denmark).

Pentz, P., 1997. *Hama: fouilles et recherches, 1931-1938; 4, pt. 1. The Medieval Citadel and its Architecture* (København: Nationalmuseet).

Petersen, A., 2005a. *The Towns of Palestine under Muslim Rule, AD 600-1600* (Oxford: Archaeopress).

Petersen, A., 2005b. What is 'Islamic' archaeology? *Antiquity* 79: 100-7.

Philip, G., Jabour, F., Beck, A., Bshesh, M., Grove, J., Kirk, A., and Millard, A., 2002. Settlement and landscape development in the Homs region, Syria: research questions, preliminary results 1999-2000 and future potential. *Levant* 34: 1-23.

Piccirillo, M., 1984. The Umayyad churches of Jordan. *Annual of the Department of Antiquities of Jordan* 28: 333-41.

Piccirillo, M., 1993. *The Mosaics of Jordan* (Amman: American Centre of Oriental Research).

Piccirillo, M. and Alliata, E., 1994. *Umm al-Rasas – Mayfa'ah I. Gli scavi del complesso di Santo Stefano* (Jerusalem: Studium Biblicum Franciscanum).

Pierobon, R., 1983-4. Gerasa I. Report of the Italian Archaeological Expedition to Jerash, Campaigns 1977-1981. Sanctuary of Artemis: Soundings in the Temple-Terrace, 1978-1980. *Mesopotamia* 18-19: 85-111.

Pirenne, H., 1939. *Mohammed and Charlemagne* trans. B. Miall (London: Unwin).

Ploug, G., 1985. *Hama: fouilles et recherches, 1931-1938; 3, pt. 1. The Graeco-Roman town* (Copenhague: Nationalmuseet).

Pollak, R., 1999. Early Islamic glass at Caesarea. In A. Raban, R. Toueg, Y.D. Arnon, R. Pollak, and A. Lester (eds), *The Richness of Islamic Caesarea* (Haifa: Reuben and Edith Hecht Museum), 24*-35*.

Redman, C.L., 2005. Resilience theory in archaeology. *American Anthropologist* 107: 70-7.

Redman, C.L. and Kinzig, A.P., 2003. Resilience of past landscapes: resilience theory, society, and the *longue durée. Ecology and Society* 7: 14. http://www.consecol.org/vol7/iss1/art14/.

Roberts, N.N., 1993. A parable of blessing: the significance and message of the Qur'anic account of 'The Companions of the Cave'. *Muslim World* 83: 295-317.

Rogers, J.M., 1974. *From Antiquarianism to Islamic Archaeology* (Cairo: Istituto italiano).

Roll, I. and Ayalon, E., 1987. The market street at Apollonia-Arsuf. *Bulletin of the American Schools of Oriental Research* 267: 61-76.

Rosen, A.M., 1999. Phytolith analysis in Near Eastern archaeology. In S. Pike and S. Gitin (eds), *The Practical Impact of Science on Near Eastern and Aegean Archaeology* (London: Archetype Publications for the Wiener Laboratory, American School of Classical Studies, Athens).

Rosen, A.M. and Weiner, S., 1994. Identifying ancient irrigation: a new method using opaline phytoliths from emmer wheat. *Journal of Archaeological Science* 21: 125-32.

Rubin, R., 1989. The debate over climate changes in the Negev, fourth-seventh centuries C.E. *Palestine Exploration Quarterly* 121: 71-8.

Sack, D., 1996. *Resafa IV. Die Große Moschee von Resafa: Rusafat Hišam* (Mainz: P. von Zabern).

Sack, D. and Becker, H., 1999. Zur städtebaulichen und baulichen Konzeption frühislamischer Residenzen in Nordmesopotamien mit ersten Ergebnissen einer Testmessung zur geophysikalischen Prospektion in Resafa-Rusafat

Hisham. In E.-L. Schwandner and K. Rheidt (eds), *Stadt und Umland: Neue Ergebnisse der archäologischen Bau- und Siedlungsforschung. Bauforschungskolloquium in Berlin vom 7. bis 10. Mai 1997 veranstaltet vom Architektur-Refereat des DAI* (Mainz: P. von Zabern), 270-86.

Saller, S.J. and Schneider, H.R., 1941. *The Memorial of Moses on Mount Nebo* (Jerusalem: Franciscan Press).

Samuel, D., 1986. Plant remains from the northwest tell at Busra. *Berytus* 34: 83-96.

Samuel, D., 2001. Archaeobotanical evidence and analysis. In S. Berthier (ed.), *Peuplement rural et aménagements hydroagricoles dans la moyenne vallée de l'Euphrate, fin VIIe-XIXe siècle: Région de Deir ez Zor-Abu Kemal, Syrie: Mission Mésopotamie syrienne, archéologie islamique, 1986-1989* (Damas: Institut français d'études arabes de Damas (IFEAD)), 347-81.

Sartre, M., 1985. *Bostra: des origines à l'Islam* (Paris: Geuthner).

Sauer, J.A., 1973. *Hesbon Pottery 1971. A Preliminary Report on the Pottery from the 1971 Excavations at Tell Hesban* (Berrien Springs, MI: Andrews University Press).

Sauer, J.A. and Magness, J., 1997. Ceramics: ceramics of the Islamic period. In E. Meyers (ed.), *The Oxford Encyclopedia of Archaeology in the Near East* (New York: Oxford University Press), 475-9.

Sauvaget, J., 1934. Le plan de Laodicée-sur-Mer. *Bulletin d'études orientales* 4: 81-114.

Sauvaget, J., 1941. *Alep. Essai sur le développement d'une grande ville syrienne, des origines au milieu du XIXe siècle* (Paris: Paul Geuthner).

Sauvaget, J., 1967. Chateaux umayyades de Syrie. Contribution a l'étude de la colonisation Arabe aux Ier et IIe siècles de l'hégire. *Revue des études islamiques* 35: 1-49.

Schaefer, J. and Falkner, R.K., 1986. An Umayyad potters' complex in the North Theatre, Jerash. In F. Zayadine (ed.), *Jerash Archaeological Project 1 1981-83* (Amman: Department of Antiquities of Jordan), 411-35.

Schick, R., 1989. The fate of the Christians in Palestine during the Byzantine-Umayyad transition, 600-750 AD. *Proceedings of the Third Symposium, the Fourth International Conference on the History of Bilad al-Sham. Bilad al-Sham During the Umayyad Period* (English Section, vol. 2): 37-48.

Schick, R., 1994. The settlement pattern of southern Jordan: the nature of the evidence. In G.R.D. King and A. Cameron (eds), *The Byzantine and Early Islamic Near East 2: Land Use and Settlement Patterns* (Princeton, NJ: Darwin Press), 133-54.

Schick, R., 1995. *The Christian Communities of Palestine from Byzantine to Islamic Rule* (Princeton, NJ: Darwin Press).

Schick, R., 1998. Palestine in the early Islamic period: luxuriant legacy. *Near Eastern Archaeology* 61: 74-108.

Shahîd, I., 1987. Heraclius and the theme system: new light from the Arabic. *Byzantion* 57: 391-406.

Shahîd, I., 1989. Heraclius and the theme system: further observations. *Byzantion* 59: 209-43.

Shahîd, I., 1995. *Byzantium and the Arabs in the Sixth Century* vol. 1.1 & 1.2 (Washington, D.C.: Dumbarton Oaks).

Shahîd, I., 2002. *Byzantium and the Arabs in the Sixth Century* vol. 2.1 (Washington, D.C.: Dumbarton Oaks)

Shboul, A.M.H., 1996. Christians and Muslims in Syria and Upper Mesopotamia in the early Arab Islamic period: cultural change and continuity. In L.

Bibliography

Olson (ed.), *Religious Change, Conversion and Culture* (Sydney: Sydney Association for Studies in Society and Culture), 74-92.

Shboul, A.M.H. and Walmsley, A.G., 1998. Identity and self-image in Syria-Palestine in the transition from Byzantine to early Islamic rule: Arab Christians and Muslims. In G. Clarke (ed.), *Identities in the Eastern Mediterranean in Antiquity* (Sydney: Mediterranean Archaeology), 255-87.

Silberman, N.A., 2001. Thundering hordes: the image of the Persian and Muslim conquests in Palestinian archaeology. In S.R. Wolff (ed.), *Studies in the Archaeology of Israel and Neighboring Lands in Memory of Douglas L. Esse* (Chicago/Atlanta: Oriental Institute/American Schools of Oriental Research), 611-23.

Smith, R.H. and Day, L.P., 1989. *Pella of the Decapolis* vol. 2 *Final Report on the College of Wooster Excavations in Area IX, the Civic Complex, 1979-1985* (Wooster, Oh.: College of Wooster).

Sodini, J.-P., Tate, G., Bavant, B., Bavant, S., Biscop, J.-L., and Orssaud, D., 1980. Déhès (Syrie du Nord). Campagnes I-III (1976-1978), Reserches sur l'habitat rural. *Syria* 57: 1-304.

Sodini, J.-P. and Villeneuve, E., 1992. Le passage de la céramique byzantine à la céramique omeyyade. In P. Canivet and J.-P. Rey-Coquais (eds), *La Syrie de Byzance à l'Islam VIIe-VIIIe siècles: actes du colloque international* (Damascus: Institut français de Damas), 195-218.

Stacey, D., 2004. *Excavations at Tiberias, 1973-1974: The Early Islamic Periods* (Jerusalem: Israel Antiquities Authority).

Stathakopoulos, D.C., 2004. *Famine and Pestilence in the Late Roman and Early Byzantine Empire: A Systematic Survey of Subsistence Crises and Epidemics* (Aldershot: Ashgate).

Tabari, trans. Hillenbrand, 1989. *The Waning of the Umayyad Caliphate (The History of al-Tabari, volume 26)* (Albany, NY: State University of New York Press).

Tate, G., 1992. *Les campagnes de la Syrie du Nord du IIe au VIIe siècle: un exemple d'expansion démographique et économique à la fin de l'Antiquité* (Paris: Paul Geuthner).

Tchalenko, G., 1953-8. *Villages antiques de la Syrie du Nord. Le massif du Bélus a l'époque romaine* (Paris: Geuthner).

Toombs, L.E., 1978. The stratigraphy of Caesarea Maritima. In R. Moorey and P. Parr (eds), *Archaeology in the Levant* (Warminster: Aris & Phillips), 223-32.

Tsafrir, Y., 1988. *Excavations at Rehovot-in-the-Negev* (Jerusalem: Institute of Archaeology, Hebrew University of Jerusalem).

Tsafrir, Y., 1993. *Ancient Churches Revealed* (Jerusalem: Israel Exploration Society).

Tsafrir, Y. and Foerster, G., 1997. Urbanism at Scythopolis-Bet Shean in the fourth to seventh centuries. *Dumbarton Oaks Papers* 51: 85-146.

Tsafrir, Y. and Holum, K.G., 1993. Rehovot-in-the-Negev. In E. Stern (ed.), *New Encyclopaedia of Archaeological Excavations in the Holy Land* vol. 4 (Jerusalem: Israel Exploration Society), 1274-7.

Tzaferis, V., 1989. *Excavations at Capernaum* (Winona Lake: Eisenbrauns).

Ulbert, T., 1986. *Resafa II. Die Basilika des Heiligen Kreuzes in Resafa-Sergiupolis* (Mainz: P. von Zabern).

Ulbert, T., 1997. Beobachtungen im Westhofbereich der Großen Basilika von Resafa. *Damaszener Mitteilungen* 6: 403-16, pls 72-6.

Urman, D. and Flesher, P.V.M., 1995. *Ancient Synagogues: Historical Analysis and Archaeological Discovery* (Leiden: Brill).

Bibliography

Uscatescu, A., 1996. *La cerámica del Macellum de Gerasa (Yaraš, Jordania)* (Madrid: Instituto del Patrimonio Histórico Español).

Vernoit, S., 1997. The rise of Islamic archaeology. *Muqarnas* 14: 1-10.

Vita-Finzi, C., 1969. *The Mediterranean Valleys* (Cambridge: Cambridge University Press).

de Vogüé, M., 1865. *Syrie centrale. Architecture civile et religieuse du Ier au VIIe siècle* (Paris: Noblet & Baudry).

de Vries, B., 1998. *Umm el-Jimal. A Frontier Town and its Landscape in Northern Jordan* vol. 1 *Fieldwork 1972-1981* (Portsmouth, RI).

de Vries, B., 2000. Continuity and change in the urban character of the Southern Hauran from the 5th to the 9th century: the archaeological evidence at Umm al-Jimal. *Mediterranean Archaeology* 13: 39-45.

Walmsley, A., 1987. The administrative structure and urban geography of the *Jund* of Filastin and the *Jund* of al-Urdunn: the cities and districts of Palestine and east Jordan during the early Islamic, 'Abbasid and early Fatimid periods. Unpublished PhD thesis, University of Sydney.

Walmsley, A., 1988. Pella/Fihl after the Islamic conquest (AD 635-c. 900): a convergence of literary and archaeological evidence. *Mediterranean Archaeology* 1: 142-59.

Walmsley, A., 1991. Architecture and artefacts from Abbasid Fihl: implications for the cultural history of Jordan. In M.A. Bakhit and R. Schick (eds), *Proceedings of the Fifth International Conference on the History of Bilad al-Sham. Bilad al-Sham during the Abbasid Period (English and French Section)* (Amman: History of Bilad al-Sham Committee), 135-59.

Walmsley, A., 1992. Fihl (Pella) and the cities of north Jordan during the Umayyad and Abbasid periods. In S. Tell, G. Bisheh, F. Zayadine, K. 'Amr, and M. Zaghloul (eds), *Studies in the History and Archaeology of Jordan* vol. 4 (Amman: Department of Antiquities of Jordan), 377-84.

Walmsley, A., 1995. Tradition, innovation, and imitation in the material culture of Islamic Jordan: the first four centuries. In K. 'Amr, F. Zayadine, and M. Zaghloul (eds), *Studies in the History and Archaeology of Jordan* vol. 5 (Amman: Department of Antiquities of Jordan), 657-68.

Walmsley, A., 1996. Byzantine Palestine and Arabia: urban prosperity in late antiquity. In N.J. Christie and S.T. Loseby (eds), *Towns in Transition: Urban Evolution in Late Antiquity and the Early Middle Ages* (Aldershot: Scolar Press), 126-58.

Walmsley, A., 1997. Ceramics and the social history of early Islamic Jordan: the example of Pella (Tabaqat Fahl). *Al-'Usur al-Wusta* 9: 1-3, 12.

Walmsley, A., 1999. Coin frequencies in sixth and seventh century Palestine and Arabia: social and economic implications. *Journal of the Economic and Social History of the Orient* 42: 324-50.

Walmsley, A., 2000. Production, exchange and regional trade in the Islamic East Mediterranean: old structures, new systems? In I.L. Hansen and C. Wickham (eds), *The Long Eighth Century. Production, Distribution and Demand* (Leiden: Brill), 265-343.

Walmsley, A., 2001. Turning East. The appearance of Islamic Cream wares in Jordan – the end of antiquity? In E. Villeneuve and P.M. Watson (eds), *La céramique byzantine et proto-islamique en Syrie-Jordanie (IVe-VIIIe siècles)* (Beyrouth: Institut français d'archéologie du Proche-Orient), 305-13.

Walmsley, A., 2004. Archaeology and Islamic studies: the development of a relationship. In K.V. Folsach, H. Thrane, and I. Thuesen (eds), *From Handaxe to Khan: Essays Presented to Peder Mortensen on the Occasion of his 70th Birthday* (Århus: Aarhus University Press), 317-29.

168

Walmsley, A., 2005. The village ascendant in Byzantine and early Islamic Jordan: socio-economic forces and cultural responses. In J. Lefort, C. Morrisson, and J.-P. Sodini (eds), *Les villages dans l'Empire byzantin (IVe-XVe siècle)* (Paris: Lethielleux), 511-22.

Walmsley, A., f.c. [2007a]. Households at Pella, Jordan: the domestic destruction deposits of the mid-eighth century. In L. Lavan, E. Swift, and M. Guidetti (eds), *Objects in Context, Objects in Use. The Archaeology of Everyday Life* (Leiden: Brill), submitted March 2005.

Walmsley, A., f.c. [2007b]. Pella, Jarash and 'Amman: old and new in the crossing to Arabia, ca. 550-750 CE. In K.G. Holum and H. Lapin (eds), *Shaping the Middle East: Cities in Transition* (Bethesda, MD: University Press of Maryland), in press.

Walmsley, A. and Grey, A., 2001. An interim report on the pottery from Gharandal (Arindela), Jordan. *Levant* 33: 139-64.

Walmsley, A.G., Macumber, P.G., Edwards, P.C., Bourke, S., and Watson, P.M., 1993. The eleventh and twelfth seasons of excavations at Pella (Tabaqat Fahl) 1989-1990. *Annual of the Department of Antiquities of Jordan* 37: 165-240.

Watson, A.M., 1983. *Agricultural Innovation in the Early Islamic World: The Diffusion of Crops and Farming Techniques, 700-1000* (Cambridge: Cambridge University Press).

Watson, P.M., 1989. Jerash bowls: study of a provincial group of Byzantine Decorated Fine ware. In F. Zayadine (ed.), *Jerash Archaeological Project 2 (1984-1988)* (Paris: Paul Geuthner), 223-53.

Watson, P.M., 1992. The Byzantine period: Byzantine domestic occupation in Areas III and IV. In A.W. McNicoll, J. Hanbury-Tenison, J.B. Hennessy, T.F. Potts, R.H. Smith, A. Walmsley, and P. Watson (eds), *Pella in Jordan 2. The Second Interim Report of the Joint University of Sydney and College of Wooster Excavations at Pella 1982-1985* (Sydney: Mediterranean Archaeology), 163-81.

Watson, P.M. and O'Hea, M., 1996. Pella Hinterland Survey 1994: preliminary report. *Levant* 28: 63-76.

Watson, P.M. and Tidmarsh, J., 1996. Pella/Tall al-Husn excavations 1993. The University of Sydney – 15th season. *Annual of the Department of Antiquities of Jordan* 40: 293-313.

Wharton, A., 2000. Erasure: eliminating the space of late ancient Judaism. In L.I. Levine and Z. Weiss (eds), *From Dura to Sepphoris: Studies in Jewish Art and Society in Late Antiquity* (Portsmouth, R.I.: Journal of Roman Archaeology), 195-214.

Wheatley, P., 2001. *The Places Where Men Pray Together: Cities in Islamic Lands, Seventh Through the Tenth Centuries* (Chicago: Chicago University Press).

Whitcomb, D., 1988a. *Aqaba 'Port of Palestine on the China Sea'* (Chicago/Amman: Al Kutba).

Whitcomb, D., 1988b. Khirbat al-Mafjar reconsidered: the ceramic evidence. *Bulletin of the American Schools of Oriental Research* 271: 51-67.

Whitcomb, D., 1989. Evidence of the Umayyad period from the Aqaba excavations. *Proceedings of the Third Symposium, the Fourth International Conference on the History of Bilad al-Sham. Bilad al-Sham during the Umayyad Period* (English Section, vol. 2): 164-84.

Whitcomb, D., 1992. Reassessing the archaeology of Jordan of the Abbasid period. In S. Tell, G. Bisheh, F. Zayadine, K. 'Amr, and M. Zaghloul (eds),

Bibliography

Studies in the History and Archaeology of Jordan vol. 4 (Amman: Department of Antiquities of Jordan), 385-90.

Whitcomb, D., 1994a. Amsar in Syria? Syrian cities after the conquest. *ARAM* 6: 13-33.

Whitcomb, D., 1994b. The *misr* of Ayla: settlement at al-'Aqaba in the early Islamic period. In G.R.D. King and A. Cameron (eds), *The Byzantine and Early Islamic Near East II. Land Use and Settlement Patterns (Papers of the Second Workshop on Late Antiquity and Early Islam)* (Princeton: Darwin Press), 155-70.

Whitcomb, D., 1995a. Islam and the socio-cultural transition of Palestine – early Islamic period (638-1099 CE). In T.E. Levy (ed.), *The Archaeology of Society in the Holy Land* (London: Leicester University Press), 488-501.

Whitcomb, D., 1995b. The misr of Ayla: new evidence for the early Islamic city. In K. 'Amr, F. Zayadine, and M. Zaghloul (eds), *Studies in the History and Archaeology of Jordan* vol. 5 (Amman: Department of Antiquities of Jordan), 277-88.

Whitcomb, D., 1999. Notes on Qinnasrin and Aleppo in the early Islamic period. *Annales archéologiques arabes syriennes (numéro spécial sur les actes du colloque international d'Alep, Alep et la route de la soie, Alep 26-30 septembre 1994)* 43: 203-9.

Whitcomb, D., 2000a. Archaeological research at Hadir Qinnasrin, 1998. *Archéologie islamique* 10: 7-28.

Whitcomb, D., 2000b. Hesban, Amman, and Abbasid archaeology in Jordan. In L.E. Stager, J.A. Greene, and M.D. Coogan (eds), *The Archaeology of Jordan and Beyond: Essays in Honor of James A. Sauer* (Winona Lake: Eisenbrauns), 505-15.

Whitcomb, D., 2001. Umayyad and Abbasid periods. In B. MacDonald, R. Adams, and P. Bienkowski (eds), *The Archaeology of Jordan* (Sheffield: Sheffield Academic Press), 503-13.

Whitcomb, D., 2002. Khirbat al-Karak identified with Sinnabra. *Al-'Usur al-Wusta* 14: 1-6.

Whitcomb, D., 2004. *Changing Social Identity with the Spread of Islam: Archaeological Perspectives* (Chicago: The Oriental Institute of the University of Chicago).

Whitcomb, D., 2006. The walls of early Islamic Ayla: defence or symbol? In H. Kennedy (ed.), *Muslim Military Architecture in Greater Syria. From the Coming of Islam to the Ottoman Period* (Leiden: Brill), 61-74.

Willcox, G., 1992. Preliminary report on plant remains from Pella. In A.W. McNicoll, J. Hanbury-Tenison, J.B. Hennessy, T.F. Potts, R.H. Smith, A. Walmsley, and P. Watson (eds), *Pella in Jordan 2. The Second Interim Report of the Joint University of Sydney and College of Wooster Excavations at Pella 1982-1985* (Sydney: Mediterranean Archaeology), 253-6.

von Willerding, U., 1984. Pflanzenreste vom FP 1 in Resafa/Nordsyrien. In M. Mackensen (ed.), *Resafa I. Eine befestigte spätantike Anlage vor den Stadtmauern von Resafa: Ausgrabungen und spätantike Kleinfunde eines Surveys im Umland von Resafa-Sergiupolis* (Mainz: P. von Zabern), 95-7.

Ye'or, B., 1996. *The Decline of Eastern Christianity under Islam. From Jihad to Dhimmitude: Seventh-Twentieth Century* (Madison, NJ: Fairleigh Dickinson University).

Index

Index

Index

176

CPSIA information can be obtained at www.ICGtesting.com
Printed in the USA
LVOW06s2121050514

384456LV00003B/17/P